BARBER'S
Turn-of-the-Century Houses
Elevations and Floor Plans

Third Edition

George F. Barber & Co.

Dover Publications, Inc., Mineola, New York

Copyright

Bibliographical Note

This Dover edition, first published in 2008, is a slightly altered republication of *Modern Dwellings: A Book of Practical Designs and Plans,* Third Edition, published by S. B. Newman & Co., Knoxville, Tennessee, in 1901.

Library of Congress Cataloging-in-Publication Data

Geo. F. Barber & Co. Architects
[Modern dwellings]
Barber's turn-of-the-century houses : elevations and floor plans / George F. Barber.—3rd ed.
p. cm.
"This Dover edition, first published in 2008, is a slightly altered republication of Modern dwellings: a book of practical designs and plans, third edition, published by S. B. Newman & Co., Knoxville, Tennessee, in 1901."
ISBN-13: 978-0-486-46527-2
ISBN-10: 0-486-46527-6
1. Architecture, Domestic—Designs and plans. I. Title.

NA7120.G37 2008
728'.370222—dc22

2007049437

Manufactured in the United States of America
Dover Publications, Inc., 31 East 2nd Street, Mineola, N.Y. 11501

MODERN DWELLINGS

—A BOOK OF—

PRACTICAL DESIGNS AND PLANS

—FOR THOSE—

WHO WISH TO BUILD OR BEAUTIFY THEIR HOMES

GEO. F. BARBER & CO., ARCHITECTS, Knoxville, Tenn.

GEO. F. BARBER, of Illinois   THOS. A. KLUTTZ, of Georgia

ESTABLISHED IN 1888 BY GEO. F. BARBER

THIRD EDITION

1901
S. B. NEWMAN & Co.
Knoxville, Tenn.

INTRODUCTORY REMARKS

PLANNING THE NEW HOME

IN PRESENTING this book of Modern Homes to the public, the idea foremost in our minds has been to produce the work in such a manner as to be of the greatest possible service to the prospective builder in formulating a satisfactory plan for his new home, giving floor plans of a convenient and practical character, and exterior designs of artistic merit in the various prevailing styles, and each thoroughly up-to-date.

We have tried to lay out for our patrons a series of handsome designs and plans, prepared from long, practical experience, in one of the most important features of our life's work—the **proper planning, designing and equipping** of the modern American home.

WHEN YOU CONSIDER THE COST OF A HOME, THE ANXIETY SPENT UPON IT, AND THE TIME IT TAKES TO BUILD IT; BUT MOST OF ALL, WHEN YOU CONSIDER HOW ENDURING ARE ALL ITS APPOINTMENTS, WHETHER GOOD OR BAD, YOU CAN NOT BUT SEE THE GREAT IMPORTANCE OF TAKING SPECIAL CARE IN ITS DEVELOPMENT.

There are thousands of houses built every year that could have been better at no greater expense. From this we see that the road to successful house-planning is no thoroughfare; it is traveled successfully only by those who have given the subject the care and study of a lifetime.

We do not make and sell stock plans; every set is developed from the ideas of the client or selected from our published designs and plans. When you desire our assistance in planning and designing your home, a **rough pencil sketch of your idea** of the arrangement of the rooms is all we need. In this way we will be able to start you right, by the proper development of the plans from your own sketches.

DEVELOPING PLANS FROM ROUGH SKETCHES

If You are Going to Build

WE SHOULD like very much to help you in developing your plans or assist you in any way we can to solve the problem, which, by the way, is a right serious one when we think about it being for a house to live in for a lifetime, perhaps. In the back of this book will be found a **specially prepared (yellow) blank sheet**, on which you will find it an easy matter to tell us fully your wants and to make a rough sketch, giving us some idea of the general arrangement of floor plans desired. From this information and sketch you send us, we will make a drawing to ¼-inch scale, making such changes and improvements as our experience and judgment dictate, and submit to you for inspection, free of cost; at the same time quote you a very low price for complete working plans, specifications, etc. If the blank above referred to has been lost, send us sketch, anyhow.

There are many people who spend years in planning a home, and in many cases many more years are spent in regretting that it is not right. We think that with our long experience we can save you many of these regrets. Let us try, at any rate.

OUR WORKING DRAWINGS

Knowing, as we do, that our working drawings, when they leave our office, go out of reach of our personal supervision, we have taken **special pains to make everything plain and easily understood.**

WHAT A SET OF OUR WORKING PLANS CONSISTS OF

Basement, or foundation; roof and floor plans; four elevations: showing front, rear and two sides; all drawn to a ¼-inch scale, with every dimension carefully figured and marked; a complete set of scale and full-sized details, for everything inside and out requiring a detail; especially prepared specifications to suit each individual order; two blank contracts and color plates for outside painting, describing their application.

Our work is so extensive, our experience extending over so wide a range of territory, and of so long duration, that we are enabled to give the most satisfactory results in every locality.

ORDERING PLANS

In ordering plans please enclose one-third the price with the order, as evidence of good faith, the remainder when the plans are finished, which will be sent C. O. D., with privilege of examination at your express office. Express charges will be prepaid when full price of plans are sent with the order. Send money by New York draft, United States or express money order.

THE ESTIMATED cost of the various houses shown in this book are based upon the experience of years of careful estimating, and will be found as accurate as possible for an average of the country, but subject to variations according to local prices and conditions; also according to the requirements of the building as provided by the plans and specifications, as ordered. **Special careful estimates, with any desired information or special sketches, will be cheerfully furnished upon request.** In the execution of our plans and specifications we provide for proper and economical methods of construction, following special instructions, and thereby insuring best possible results. Our experience extends over a number of years of the most successful endeavor throughout the United States and many foreign countries.

For the designs shown in this book the estimates of cost for each building have been revised up-to-date—1901.

Is not the character of work shown in this volume sufficient evidence that we can do the work of planning your home satisfactorily, and perhaps give you something different from what you see around you every day? That is sometimes an important point. It portrays the excellent character of work our plans will produce when properly carried out by a competent builder. And in considering the building of a home, is it not economy on your part to get your plans where you are sure of satisfactory results? Will not the general appearance of your home, and an interior arrangement prepared by those of the widest experience be points it will pay you to consider? Kindly let us hear from you.

A beautiful and complete home is the dream of every American housewife. A home, with an exterior of pleasing design, beautiful and correct in every minute detail, and an interior of faultless arrangement, planned to greet the eye at every turn with new thoughts of surprising fitness. All are susceptible of the most artistic embellishment in furnishings and decorations the deft hand of the skillful mistress can bestow upon them. Such may be and should be the **Modern American Home.**

The designs in this book are figured to be complete in all modern appointments, except heating, mantels, grates and attics.

LEE, GOOCHLAND CO., VA., June 18, 1900.

Geo. F. Barber & Co.:

GENTLEMEN—You certainly deserve the high encomiums pronounced upon you *everywhere* as architects for your artistic taste, fair and courteous treatment, and very reasonable charge.

Let me add that I wish my name placed upon the list of your admirers and friends, and that you shall certainly have whatever future patronage I may have to bestow in your line.

Very truly yours,

JOSEPH R. ANDERSON.

BUENA VISTA, VA., October 2, 1900.

Geo. F. Barber & Co.:

GENTLEMEN—It is with great pleasure I acknowledge the receipt of your preliminary drawings, with floor plans and front elevation. I do not believe it possible to improve upon them, and you may count on my order for plans. I say this because I have at my home (and have been studying) a good stack of books from nearly every other architect, and I have concluded that you, and only you, can furnish me with what I want.

Very truly,

W. P. LEE.

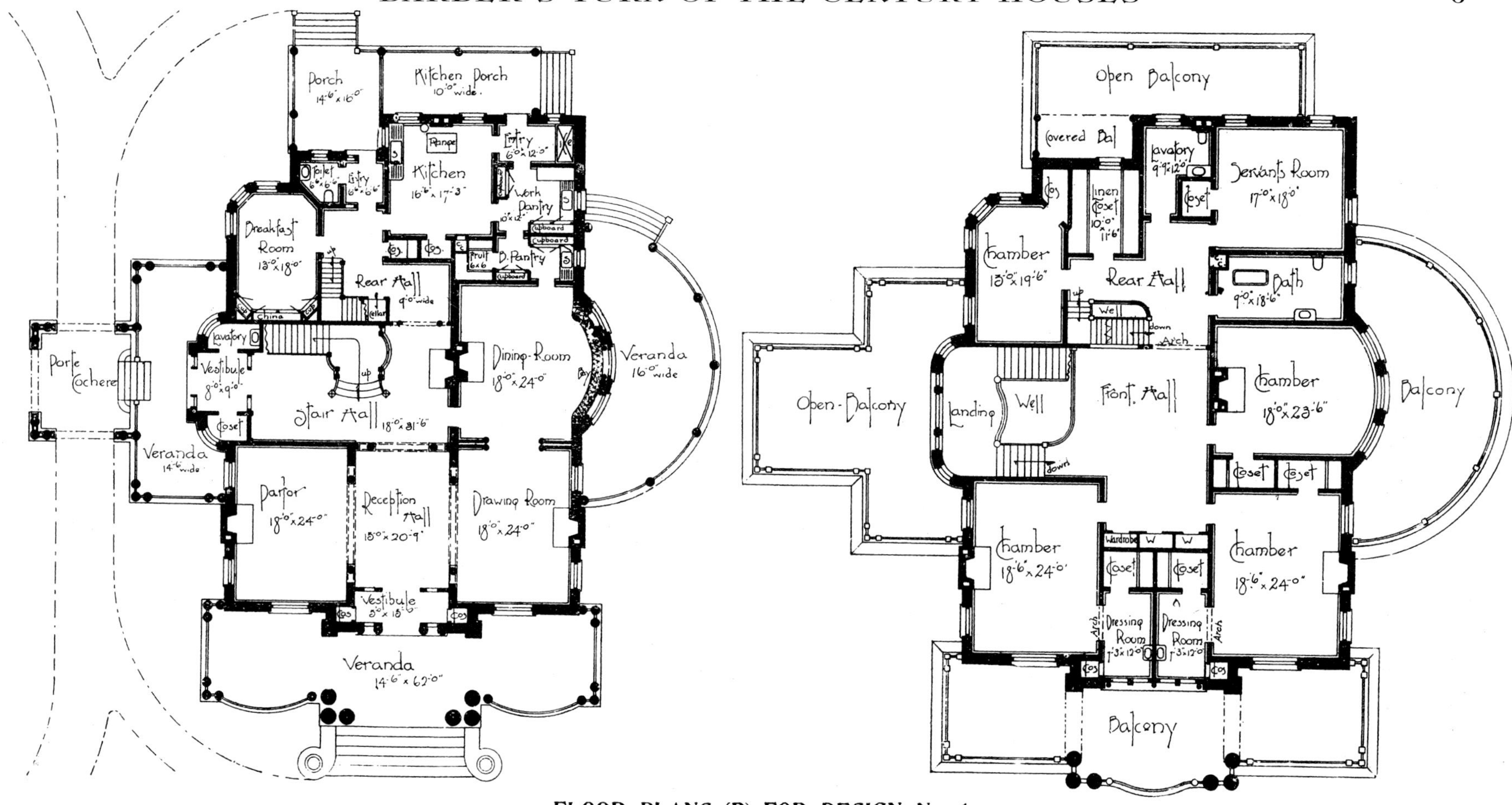

FLOOR PLANS (B) FOR DESIGN No. 1

THIS DELIGHTFUL plan for a large and elegant home, costing from $30,000 to $40,000 has been developed from the many valuable suggestions coming to us from time to time from many prominent ladies in all parts of the United States.

The dining-room is large and handsome, the bay window having especially designed fittings, upholstered seat, etc. Connected with this is the drawing-room, the doors sliding between ornate columns on either side of the opening, and the elegance of the relation of the two front rooms and the front hall will be seen at once. The stair hall, with its vestibule, lavatory and exit to porte-cochère, is all one could desire. The breakfast room is located for convenience to the kitchen, and children coming down the back stairs can reach it without appearing in any other part of house.

A spacious kitchen enters from the rear through a vestibule, in which is located the ice-box, thus away from the heat of the stove, and, at the same time, convenient to the work pantry; this in turn connected with the butler's pantry, off from which is a dark fruit closet.

The second floor is equally well arranged. Ball or billiard rooms can be located in the basement or attic. The exterior walls are of stone and brick, beautifully harmonized, with red slate for the roof, plate glass, best of hardware, and plumbing throughout.

DESIGN No 1. A MOST BEAUTIFUL HOME OF THE GEORGIAN TYPE—(CLASSIC COLONIAL) *Geo. F. Barber & Co., Arcts.*

COST (HANDSOMELY FINISHED) $30,000 TO $40,000

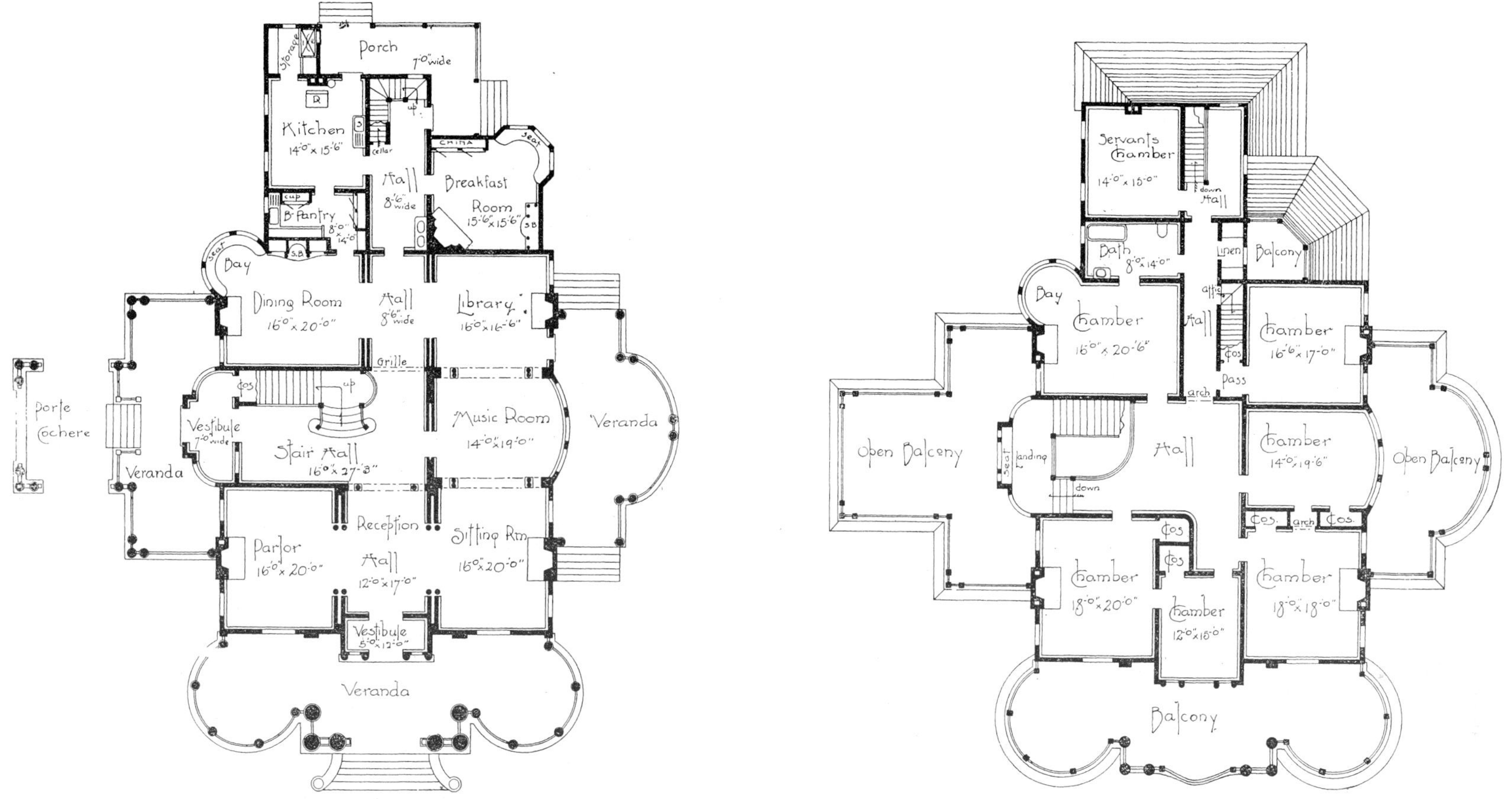

FLOOR PLANS (A) FOR DESIGN No. 1

IN THIS magnificent rendering of Georgian or classic Colonial architecture, as applied to a modern American home, we have gone far enough to include every possible feature of elegance and usefulness to be obtained in a house of this cost. The porches are of beautiful classic design and all of the exterior is nicely treated.

For the interior an excellent opening of rooms across the front, viz.: parlor, hall and sitting-room, of a certain character of treatment; then the beautiful throwing together of the rooms along the right of hall, viz.: sitting-room, music-room and library in a different style, in which are artistically employed three double-columned beams, making one grand stretch of rooms of 53 feet in extent.

Across the back hall another series of rooms—library, hall and dining-room—each capable of being separated or cut off by sliding doors. In all a grand circuitous sweep of beautiful rooms.

Height of stories are 12 feet and 11 feet—a full basement and finished attic. Complete in every detail. Further particulars on application.

FLOOR PLANS FOR DESIGN No. 2

A MORE complete home for a country or seaside place is hard to find. A wide, spacious hall and cool, airy rooms, with a 10-foot porch on three sides, makes a combination suggestive of ease and comfort. The double parlor is elegant, as are all double rooms. The second story has six pleasant rooms, besides bath, closets, and a large sewing-room.

Everything is in first-class shape for a matchless Southern home. The cellar is located under the back part of house. Brick foundation. Shingles are used on the second story and roof. Light Colonial colors are used for the exterior painting, producing a lasting and beautiful effect.

The width of front is 67 feet over porches. Stories are 11 feet and 10 feet, respectively, but may be increased to 12 and 11 feet when preferred for Southern locality.

There are two bath-rooms provided, but a private bath may be had on second floor in place of dressing-room. The lavatory under the front stairs, first floor, saves going to any other room to wash. The outside treatment of columns, grilles and seats assists in making the first floor most delightful all through. Further particulars on application.

DESIGN No. 2. **SUBURBAN OR COUNTRY HOME—(COLONIAL)** *Geo. F. Barber & Co., Arcts.*

COST, $7,500 TO $8,500

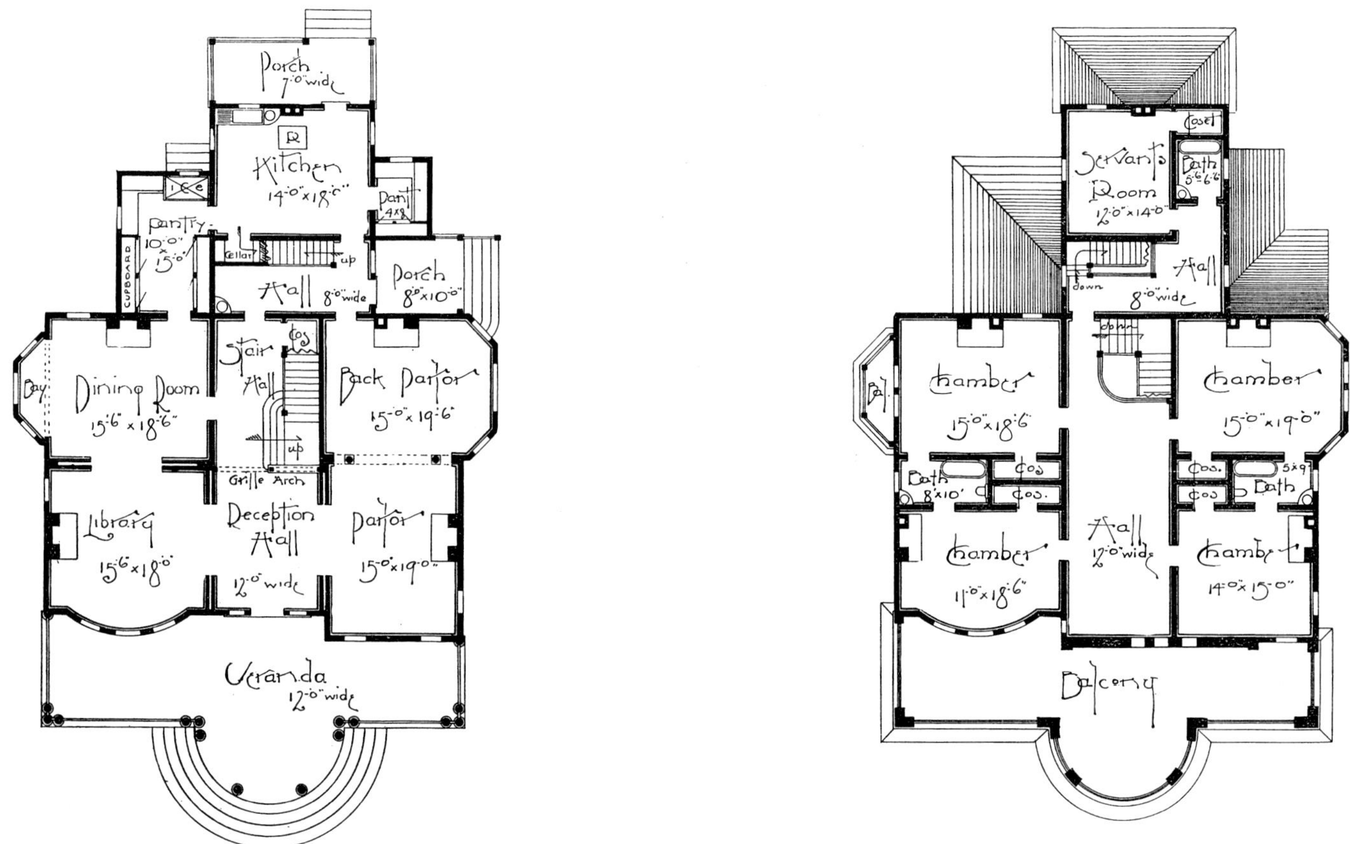

FLOOR PLANS FOR DESIGN No. 3

A COLONIAL RESIDENCE, prepared for erection in New Orleans. The feature is the wide, central hall, with spacious rooms on either side, all thrown together, making almost one continuous room of the first floor. The second story is thrown into suites, with baths between. Weather-boarding is used for exterior walls, shingles for the roof.

The exterior design presents many attractive Colonial features, such as windows, doors, etc. The stories are 11 feet and 10 feet high, with handsome Colonial interior designing for casing, stairs, etc. The mantels are placed for best effect. Cellar under kitchen and back hall. Width 55 feet 6 inches, length 78 feet, over porches.

A heavy beam divides the double parlor, with paneled effect supported by Ionic columns. An appropriate grille spans the hall at the stair case, a feature of handsome effect from the front door. Further particulars on application.

DESIGN No. 3. **SUBSTANTIAL COLONIAL HOME** *Geo. F. Barber & Co., Arcts.*

COST, $6,000 TO $7,000

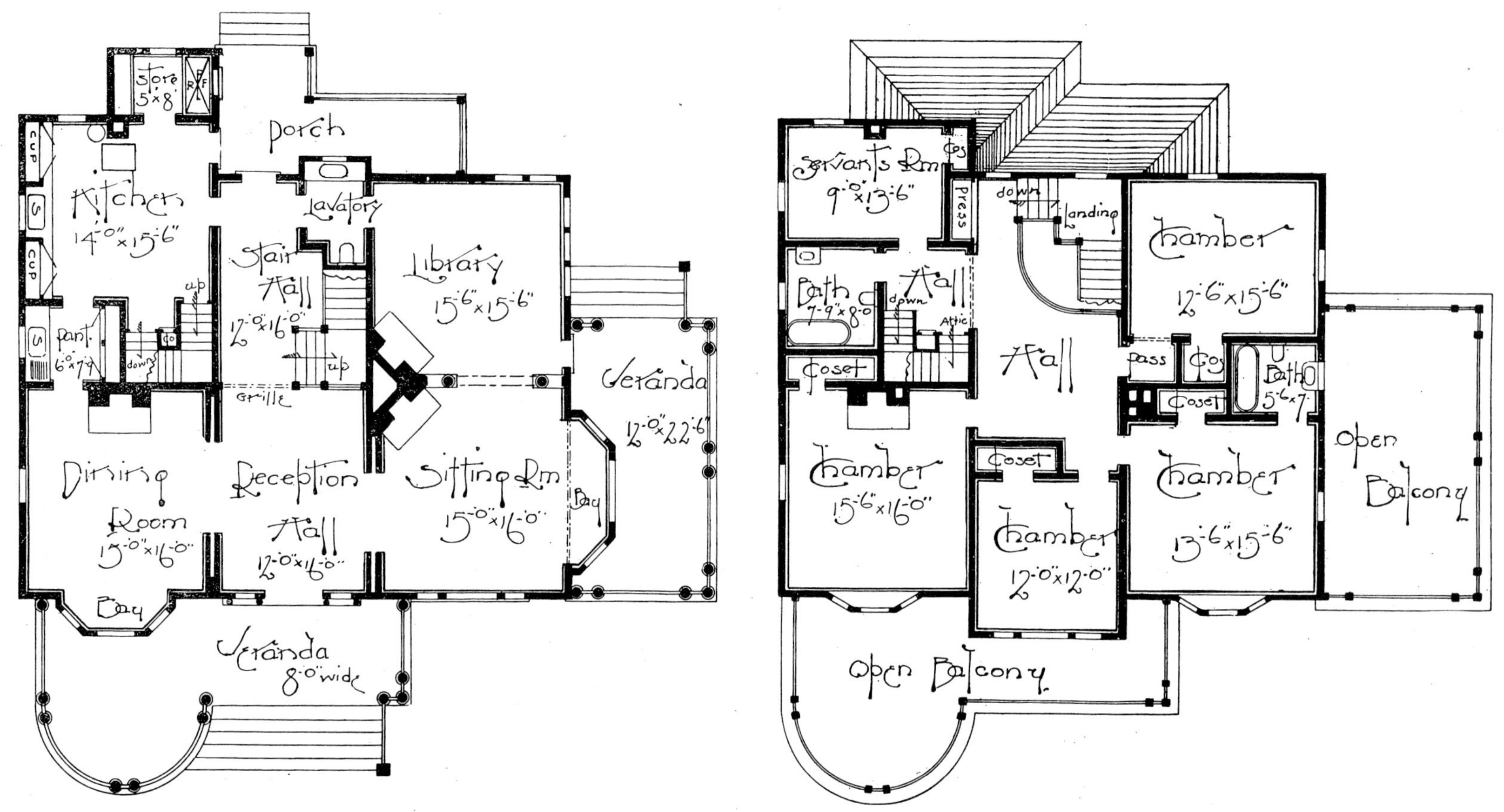

FLOOR PLANS FOR DESIGN No. 4

THE PLANS for this exquisite specimen of Colonial work have been prepared for a number of persons with various changes in the arrangement of the floor plans, sometimes cutting the price down to $4,000 and again raising it to $8,000 or even $10,000. The beam and column effect between the sitting-room and library is an artistic means by which we obtain one large room 15 feet by 32 feet 6 inches.

The plans contain a wide, central hall, provided with a treatment of stairs and grille work of unique design. The dining-room occurs at the front of the building, and is entered from the kitchen through the butler's pantry, while in the kitchen on either side of the sink are arranged ample cupboards. The cellar is under the back part of the house, containing steam boiler. Both inside and outside cellar stairs are provided.

The house is frame, using 2 x 6 studding for the better accommodation of inside sliding and Venetian blinds. All features have been carefully studied and everything is specified to make the house complete. Size 57 feet front by 55 feet deep, over porches; stories 10 feet, and 9 feet 2 inches.

The spacious porch on the right side may be repeated on the left with excellent effect, or may be eliminated entirely when cost is a consideration. The outside walls of this house may be covered with rough cast or weather-boarding, or may be built of brick or stone.

DESIGN No. 4.

MODERN COLONIAL HOME

COST $5,000 TO $5,700

Geo. F. Barber & Co., Arcts.

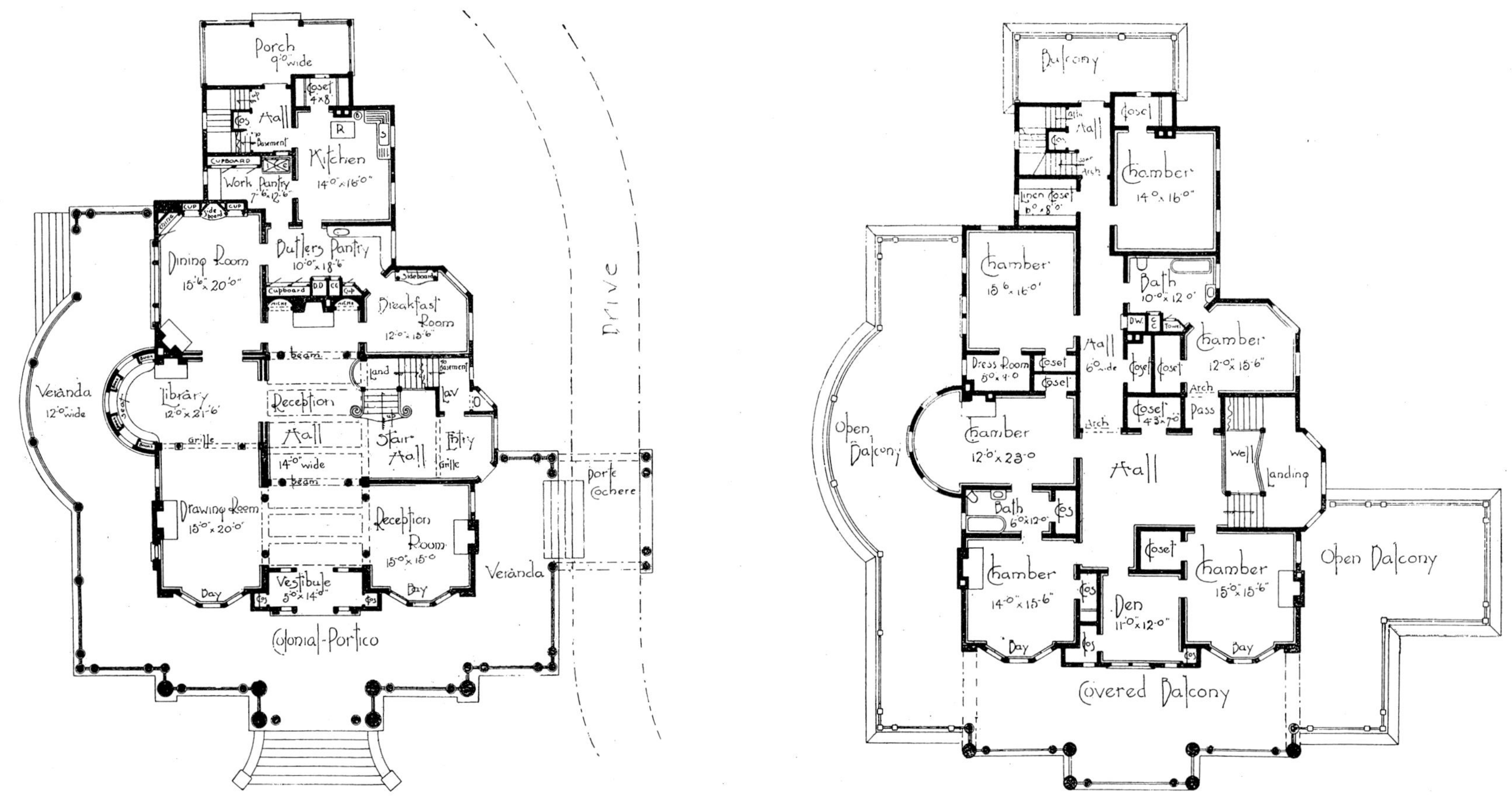

FLOOR PLANS (A) FOR DESIGN No. 5

THIS HOME was erected at Seattle, Wash., on a slightly more expensive scale for $22,450. A home, the emblem of everything substantial, beautiful and elevating in character. Elaborately finished throughout. Actual cost from builder's estimate. A study of the floor plans will reveal many desirable features in this classic home. The dining-room contains a handsome built-in china closet and side-board.

A massive front porch of true Grecian proportions constitutes a main front feature; extending through this and around the house is a 12-foot veranda. Through the hall from the front door is a beautiful vista, extending to a rich Colonial mantel beyond, through a handsome treatment of columns, beams and paneled ceilings.

The library has a circular bay built of stone to the second floor, with the four deep spaces between the windows finished in bookcases, fitted with art glass doors. The side entrance to the hall leads to a convenient lavatory; thence by descent to a ball or billiard-room below.

The second floor is liberally supplied with sleeping-rooms, closets, baths, etc., nearly all closets containing large dress drawers. Stories are 11 and 10 feet. Basement 8 feet 6 inches. Further particulars on application.

DESIGN No. 5. A STATELY HOME OF THE BEAUTIFUL GEORGIAN TYPE—(CLASSIC COLONIAL) *Geo. F. Barber & Co., Arcts.*

COST, (TASTEFULLY FINISHED) $18,000 TO $20,000

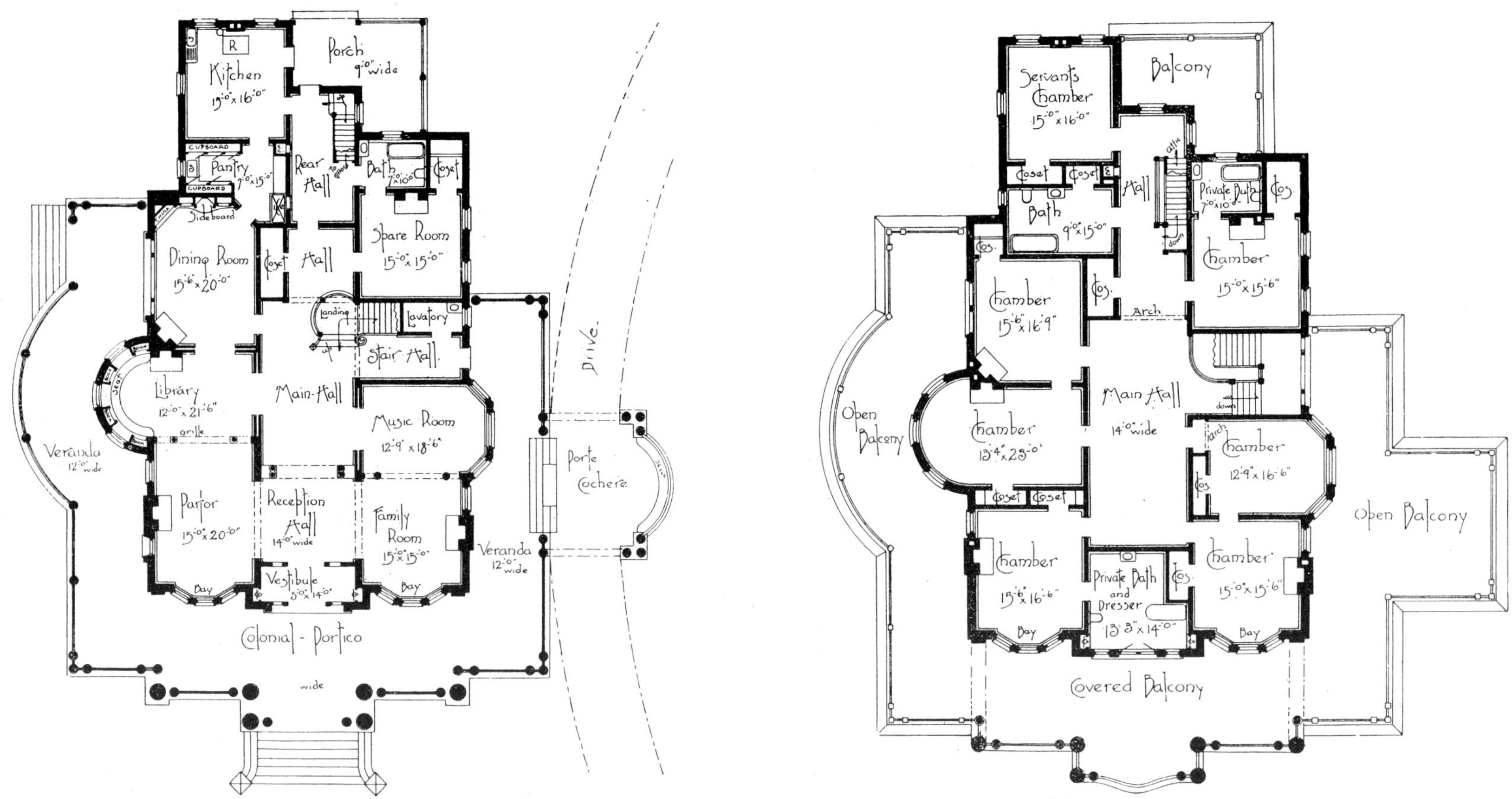

FLOOR PLANS (B), IN BRICK FOR DESIGN No. 5

THE ABOVE plans show some changes suggested by a Southern lady, viz.: the house to be built of brick, two rooms on the right of hall in front of stair hall, instead of one, the same to be separated by columns, the front one to be used as a family-room and the back part as a music-room. The hall fire-places removed and a closet instead, with hall extending on through the house. A spare bed-room, with bath and closet, on first floor, the main porch extending further along the right side. All splendid suggestions—the excellence of this arrangement induces its publication here.

One large additional chamber on second floor is obtained, and a fine private bath over front hall, as well as a private bath over rear bath below, and a public bath off from back hall. The price of this house, in brick, will be about the same as plan No. 1, but varying according to the price of brick used.

DESIGN No. 5. **A STATELY GEORGIAN HOME** *Geo. F. Barber & Co., Arcts.*

DIRECT FRONT VIEW OF DESIGN SHOWN ON PAGE 15

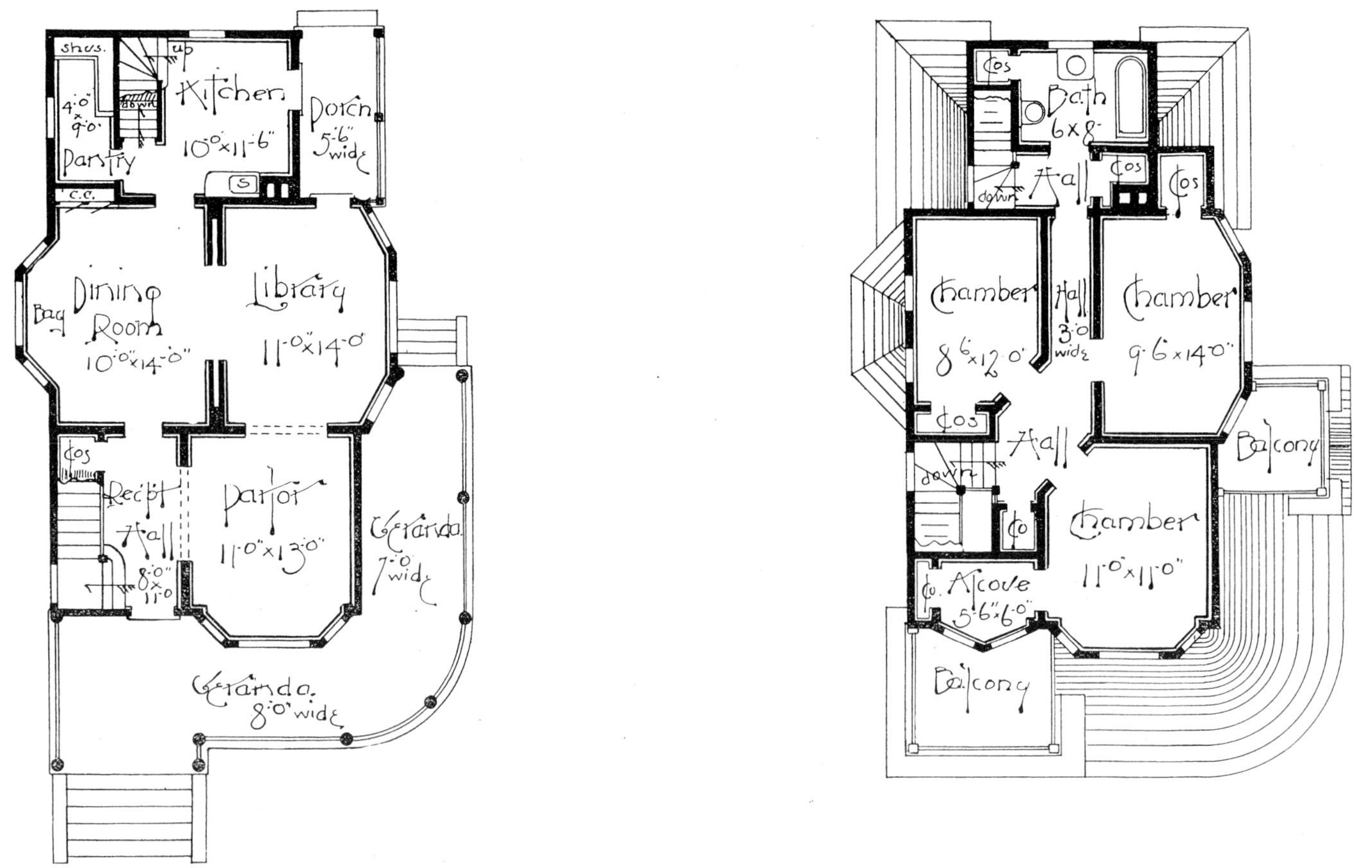

FLOOR PLANS FOR DESIGN No. 6

THIS artistic home was designed for erection in a Northern city, hence its construction is such as to stand against winter storms of the most rigid climate. One will see in this a happy combination of rooms, a large and commodious piazza, and an air of unusual taste in the exterior design. This is a house that can be enlarged to almost any dimensions and preserve the exterior features.

Back and front stairs are provided. A small cellar is under the kitchen and one other room. The hall and parlor are in oak finish; the rest of entire house is in pine, stained or natural. The width of house is 29 feet 6 inches. Stories are 9 feet, and 8 feet 2 inches, respectively.

Grates are not provided, as the house is intended to be heated by a furnace. A grate in the library, where the kitchen chimney is shown, and one in the parlor, centre of right-hand wall, would be very beneficial in giving heat in mild weather. And small stoves, or even grates, which are better, could be used upstairs.

DESIGN No. 6.

SUBURBAN BEAUTY—MODIFIED COLONIAL

COST, $2,300 TO $2,600

Geo. F. Barber & Co , Arcts.

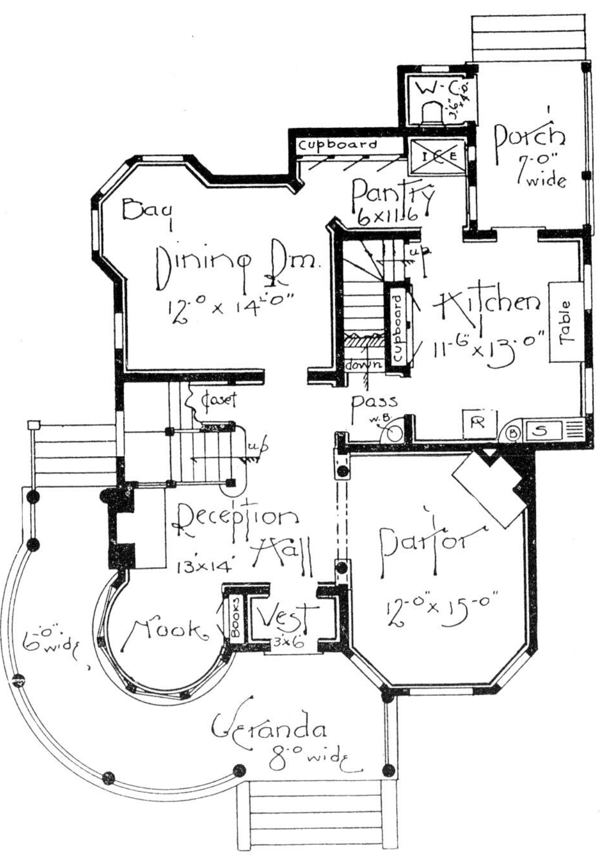

FIRST FLOOR OF PLAN No. 1

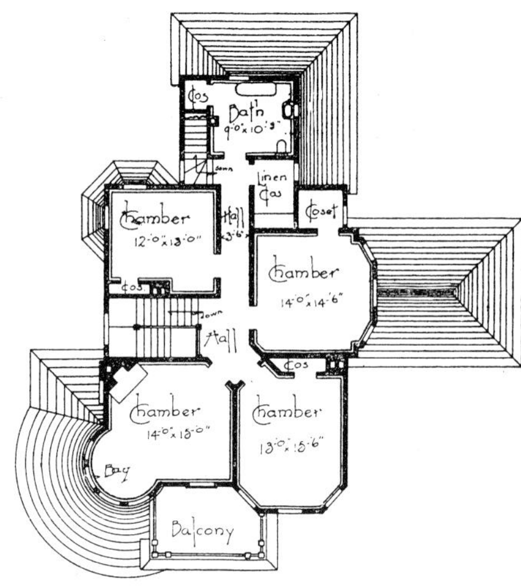

SECOND FLOOR OF PLAN No. 2

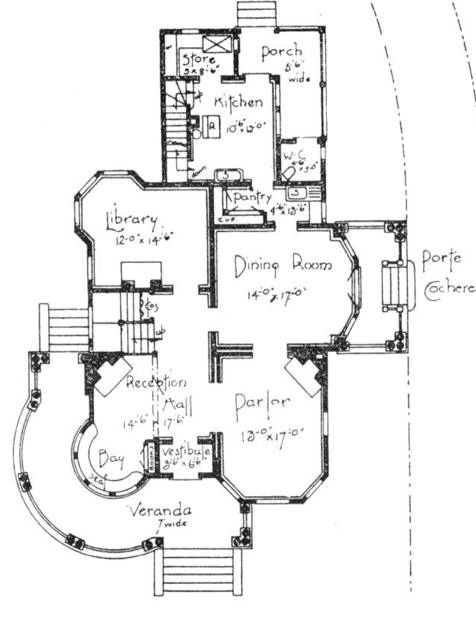

FIRST FLOOR OF PLAN No. 2

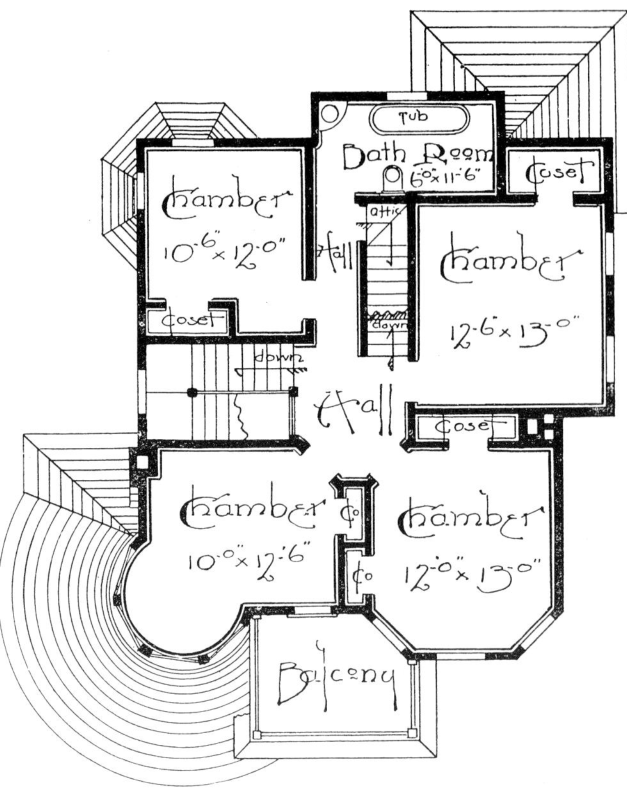

SECOND FLOOR OF PLAN No 1

THIS HOUSE—Colonial in style—has many features of artistic merit not possible to show in the cut. The entrance hall is a charming reception-room, with its artistic staircase, handsome grille, wood mantel, circular bay with its upholstered seat, a convenient bookcase and the indispensable coat closet and neatly finished vestibule. Off the hall is a small wash-room, with entrance to cellar convenient both to hall and kitchen. Many other features will present themselves.

FLOOR PLANS FOR DESIGN No. 7

The cellar is under kitchen only—stone foundation—roof and side walls above first story shingled. All other parts first-class throughout. Stories 9 feet 6 inches, and 9 feet. Cellar 7 feet for both plans.

A mantel and grate in the dining-room, and one or two grates in the second story rooms, would make them more cheerful and convenient, as a mantel is always a great convenience as well as an article of embellishment to a room.

DESIGN No. 7. A HANDSOME SUBURBAN HOME—(COLONIAL) *Geo. F. Barber & Co., Arcts.*

COST, $3,000 TO $3,300 ON PLAN NO. 1
COST $4,000 TO $4,500 ON PLAN NO. 2

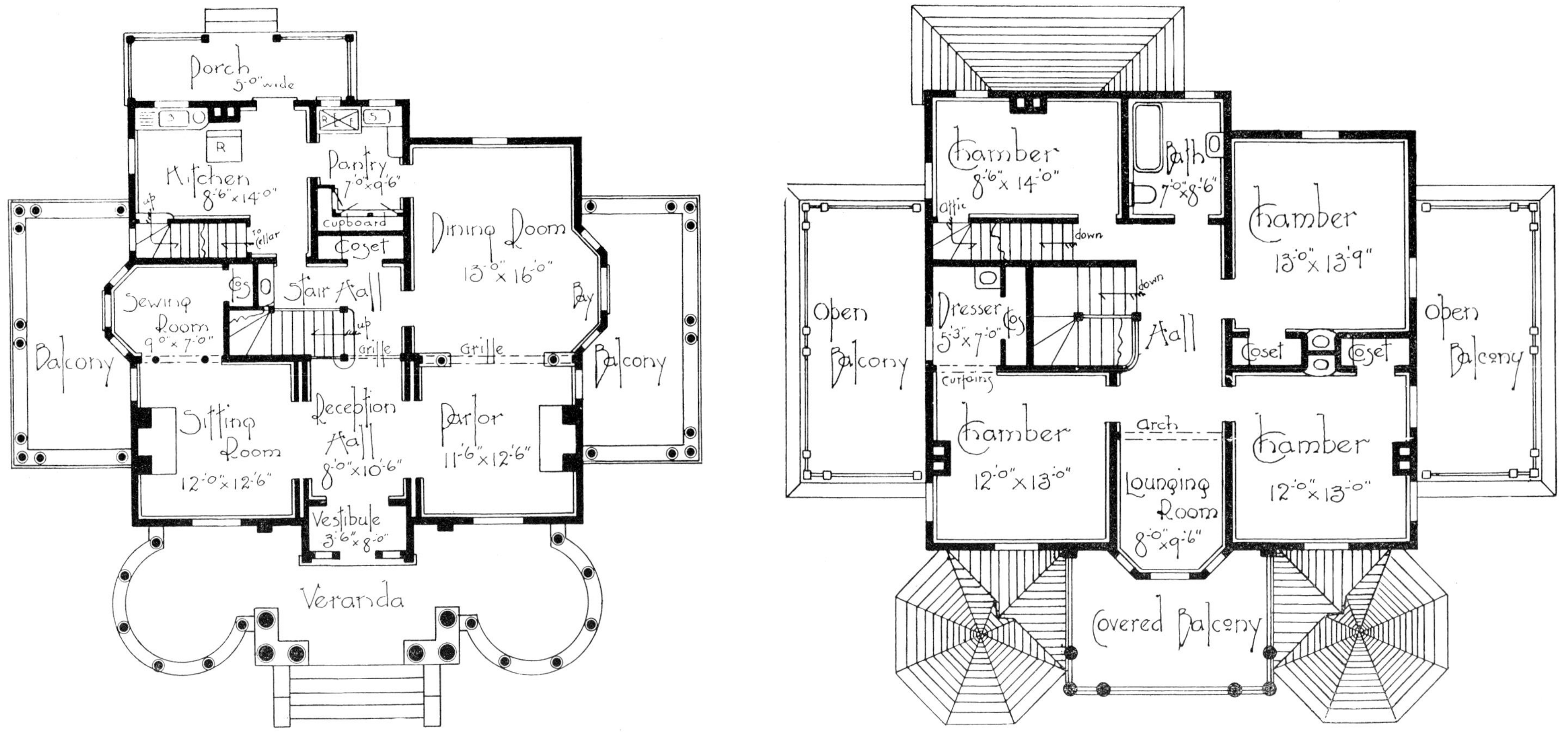

FLOOR PLANS FOR DESIGN No. 8

WITH proper treatment the Georgian style of architecture can be applied to homes of moderate cost with beautiful effect, as here shown. The plan is beautiful indeed. The front porch, handsome in itself, with stately classic treatment, is in beautiful contrast with the two square side porches. The arrangement of the rooms will appeal to every one of taste as complete in every detail.

A convenient coat closet at the rear of hall, with a marble set wash bowl near by under the stairs, filling out the space back of the sewing-room closet. Any desirable changes can be made to suit. By enlarging the house may be made to cost from $8,000 to $12,000. The stories are 10 feet and 9 feet. Width over porches, 56 feet. The house is complete in every modern appointment.

A house of similar design and plan will be found on pages 24 and 25, which may be more desirable to some tastes, but both are excellent examples of Colonial designing. Further particulars will be given on application.

DESIGN No. 8. A MODERATE PRICED HOME OF THE GEORGIAN TYPE—(CLASSIC COLONIAL) *Geo. F. Barber & Co., Arcts.*

COST, $4,800 TO $5,200

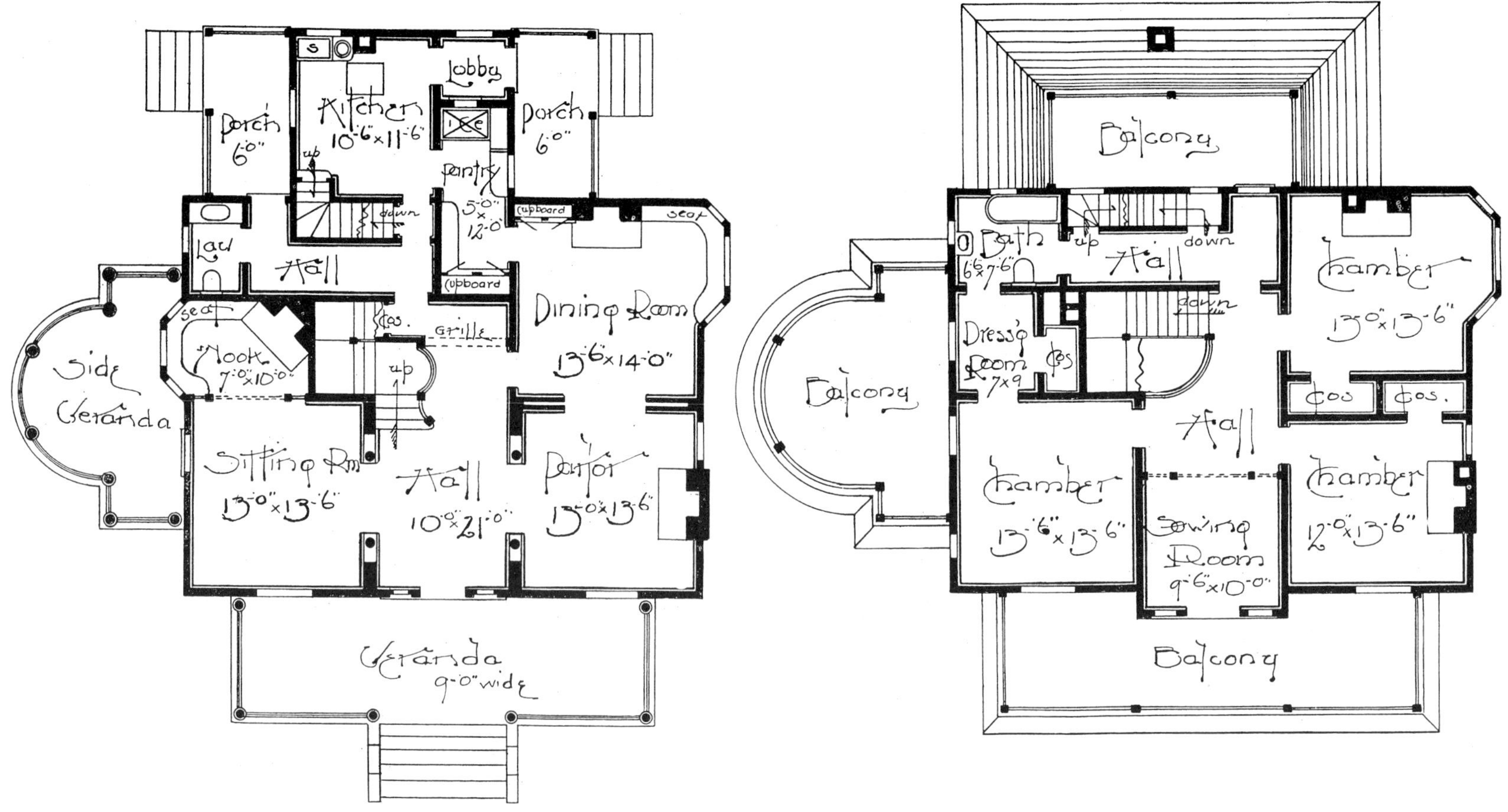

FLOOR PLANS FOR DESIGN No. 9

THE ABOVE Colonial home was designed to meet the demand for something both artistic and convenient. The arrangement of the two front rooms and hall is not only convenient but beautiful in its effect. The dining-room is also ideal. The convenience of the rear part of the house will be apparent. The refrigerator is so located in the pantry as to be iced from the lobby, thus saving the annoyance of the ice man going through the house. The lavatory off the back hall is very desirable.

The front porch as well as the side one are features of merit. The nook, with its fire-place and seats, cut off from the main room by a beautiful grille, gives a cosy effect and is quite an addition to the sitting-room. The house is finished complete in every modern appointment.

With cellar under back part of house, stone foundation, shingle roof, and a generous amount of hardwood interior finish, this house can be built in most any locality for the price given. Width over all, 55 feet. Stories 9 feet 6 inches, and 9 feet, respectively. The exterior, though plain, presents a very highly artistic effect. Stories may be made higher or size of rooms changed to suit any locality or requirements.

DESIGN No. 9. **A BEAUTIFUL GEORGIAN HOME OF LOW COST—(CLASSIC COLONIAL)** *Geo F. Barber & Co., Arcts.*

COST, $4,200 TO $4,600

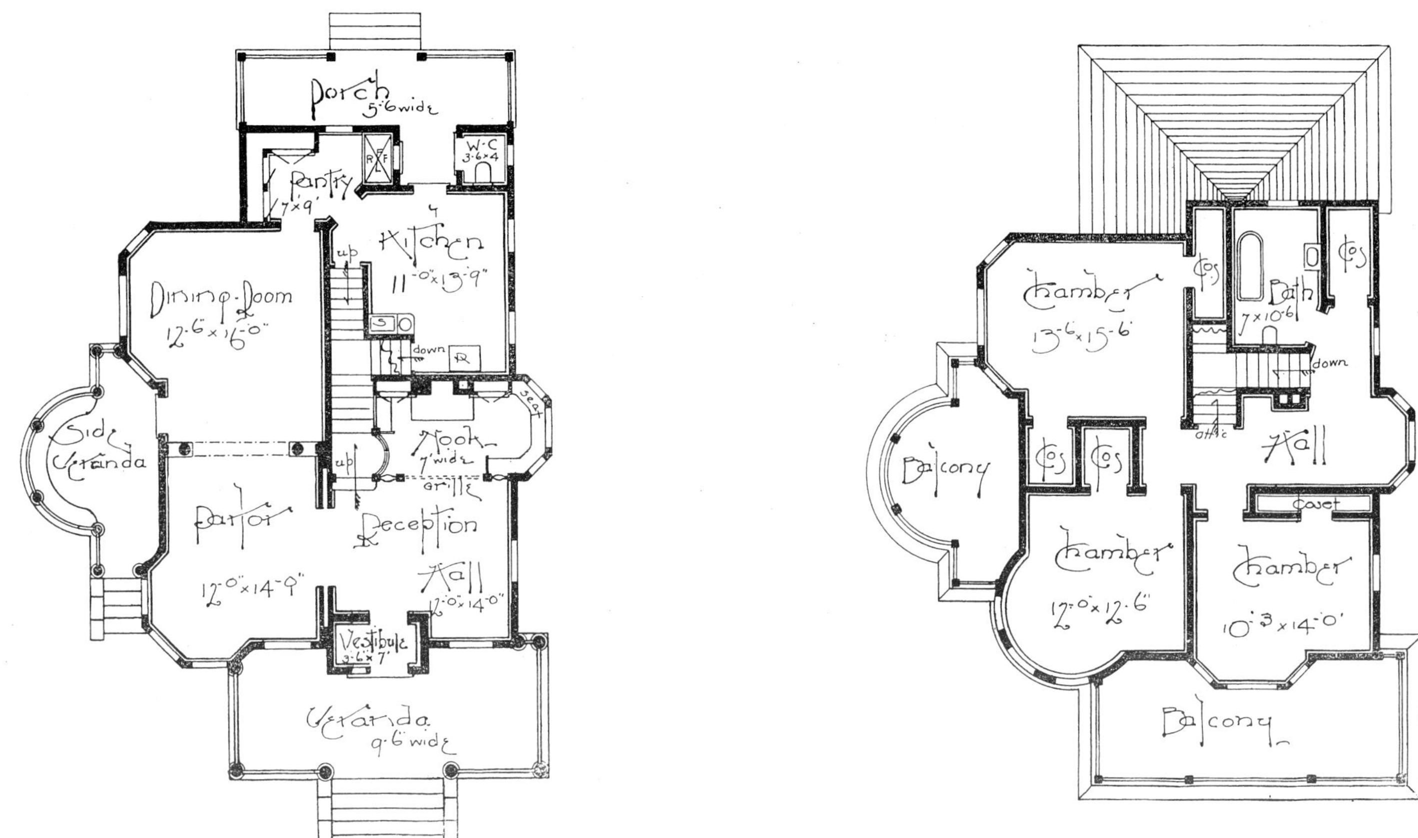

FLOOR PLANS FOR DESIGN No. 10

A MOST strikingly beautiful example of Colonial Renaissance, planned with a reception hall, artistically combined with a convenient library nook, and separated from the main hall by a grille of most charming pattern, in combination with seat, staircase, etc., handsomely placed for unique effects. The mantel is low, the bookcases being carried up on either side and across the top over the mantel, taking the place of a glass or mirror. The doors are of clear glass, neatly leaded in patterns. A beautiful combination, indeed.

A paneled beam, supported with Ionic columns, divides the parlor and dining-room. The side porch, a beautiful place for evening recreation, is reached from the latter room.

The hall and two main rooms are finished in oak. The back stairs unite with the front ones, but may be carried up separately, if desired, by shortening the bath-room on second floor. Width of house over porches is 41 feet 6 inches, length 54 feet. Stories are 9 feet 6 inches, and 9 feet.

Cellar under kitchen and dining-room. Roof slated, second story shingled. The cost covers everything but heating, and is complete in all modern requirements.

DESIGN No 10. A CHARMING HOME FOR ANY PLACE—(COLONIAL RENAISSANCE) *Geo. F. Barber & Co., Arcts.*

COST, $3,200 TO $3,600

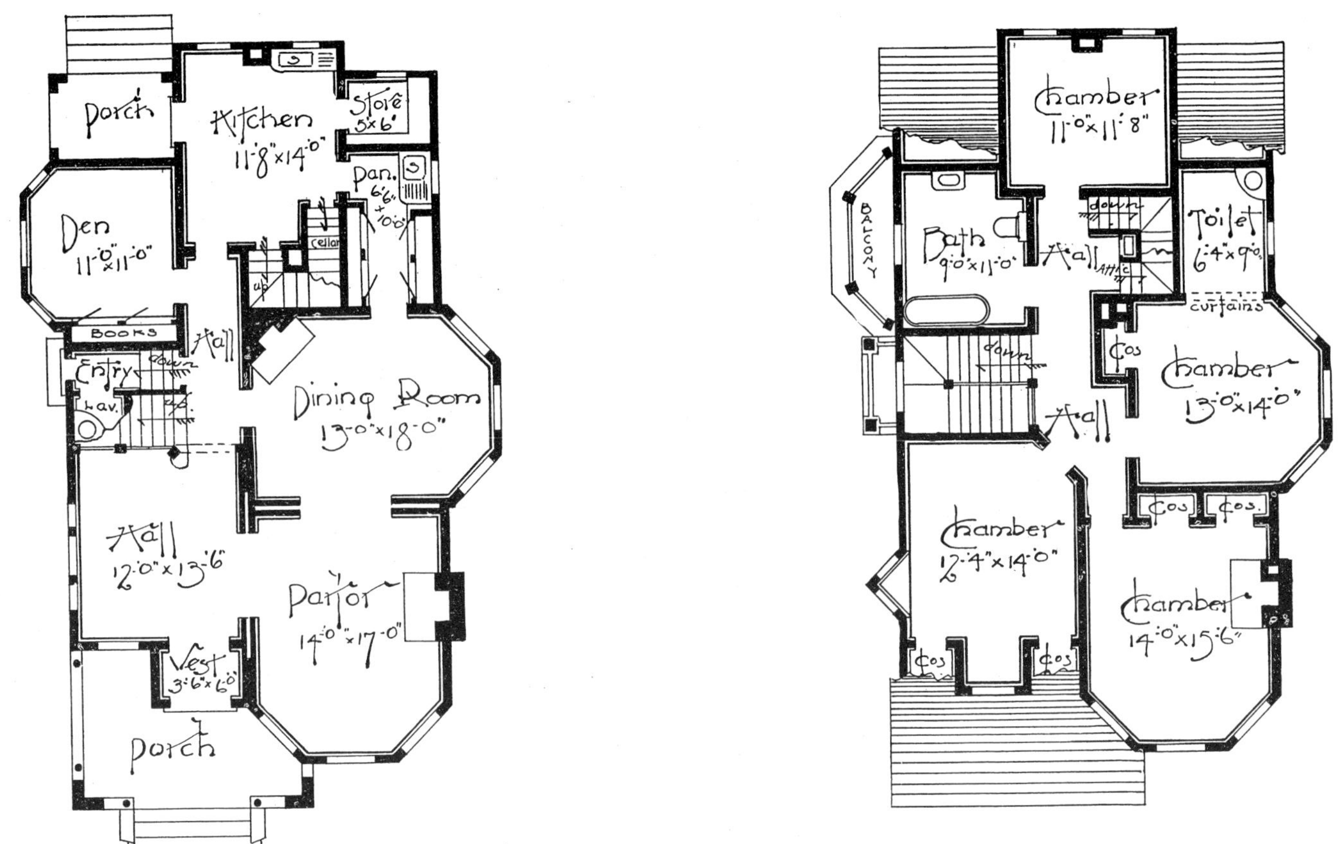

FLOOR PLANS FOR DESIGN No. 11

A PICTURESQUE Colonial home, with floor plans of many convenient features. The exterior is simple, avoiding all unnecessary expensive ornaments, relying upon beautiful lines for artistic effect. The den back of main hall may be employed as a small library or sewing-room, answering admirably for either.

The interior is treated simply, only two rooms, the parlor and hall, being in hardwood, the rest in native pine. Foundation is of stone. Good cellar under main part. Entire house from ground up, including roof, is shingled. The house can be built on a 40-foot lot. Width 36 feet, length 54 feet, over porches. Stories are 10 feet and 9 feet 2 inches high.

By a descent under the front stairs to the side entrance we get room for a lavatory that saves going to the kitchen or up to the bath-room to wash.

DESIGN No. 11. COTTAGE BY THE SEA—(COLONIAL) *Geo. F. Barber & Co., Arcts.*

COST, $3,800 TO $4,200

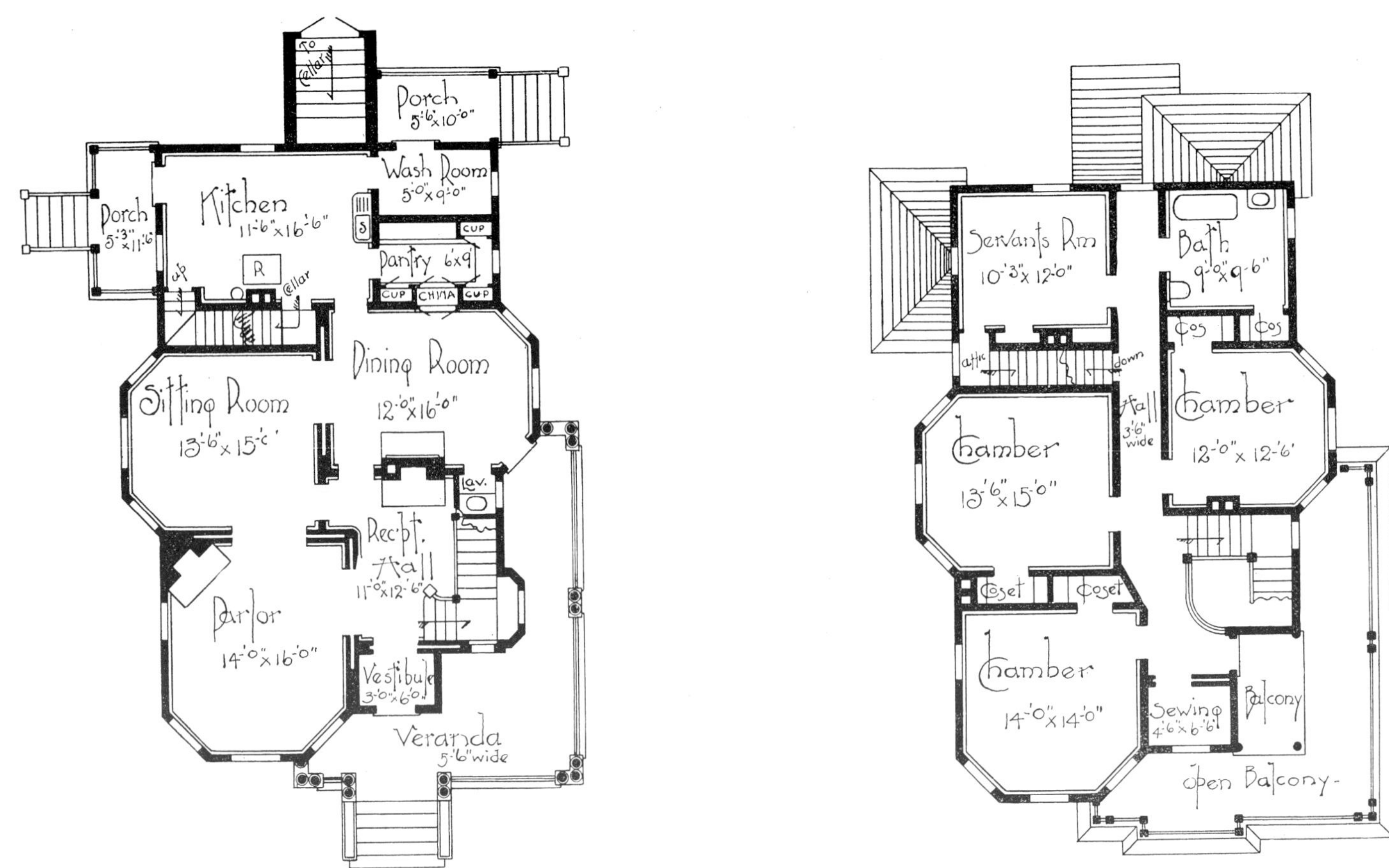

FLOOR PLANS FOR DESIGN No. 12

THIS COLONIAL design was recently erected in Wisconsin. The finish throughout is good, above the average. The dining-room has a parquette border; the vestibule and bath-room have tile floors, and a number of rooms are finished in hardwood. There is a good cellar, stone foundation, cypress shingled roof, and all first-class work.

Size 36 x 54.6. First story 9 feet; second story 8 feet, 2 inches. These heights may be changed as required. The plan is a happy combination of convenient rooms. The porch and balcony are elegant features, and a special study was given to get good results in every particular.

Grates are provided in the parlor and hall. The dining-room has a mantel with hearth and facing and summer front, but no grate. A grate or two on the second floor would not come amiss.

DESIGN No. 12. **WISCONSIN HOME—(COLONIAL)** *Geo. F. Barber & Co., Arcts.*

COST, $3,800 TO $4,200

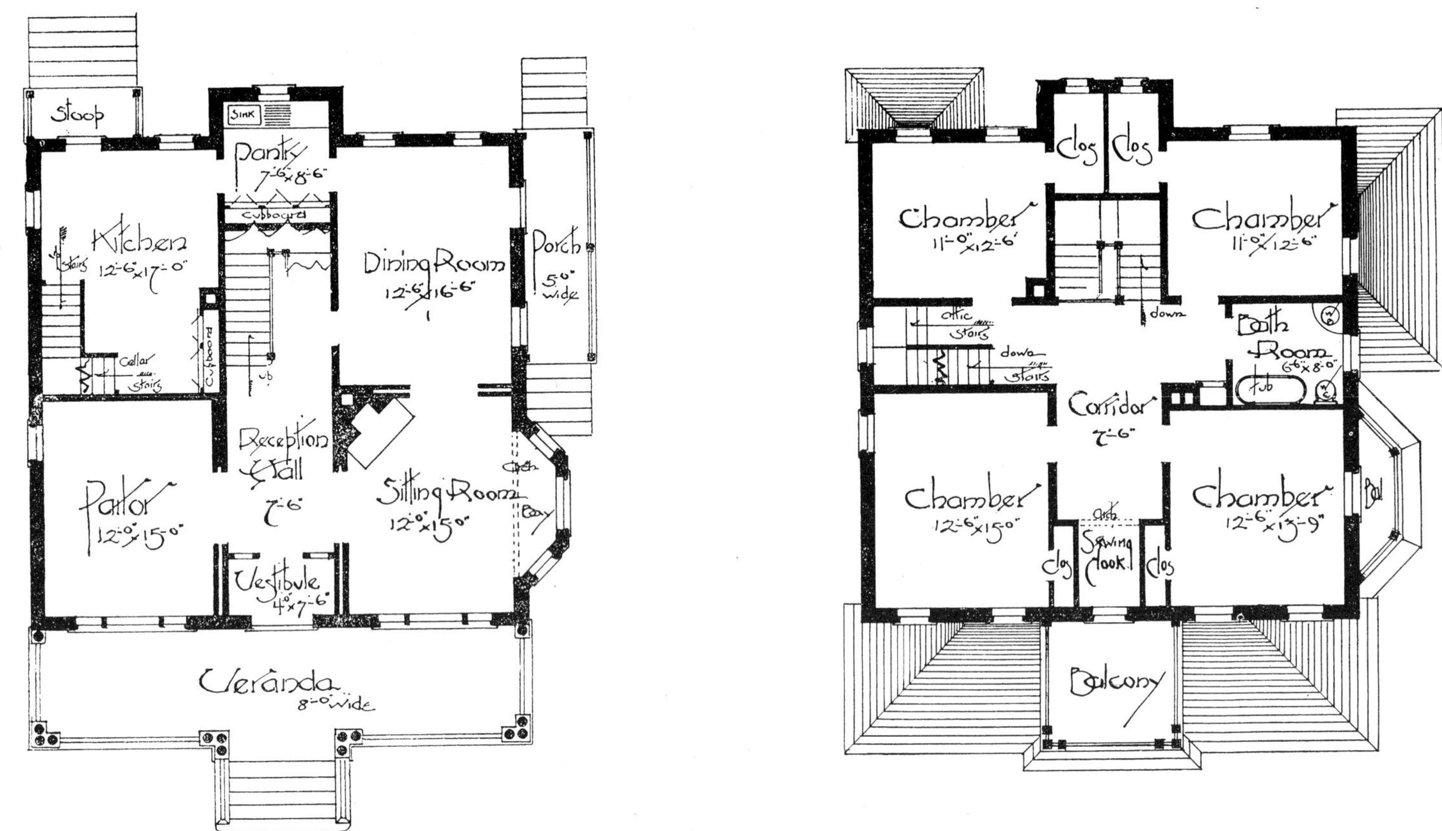

FLOOR PLANS FOR DESIGN No. 13

AN INEXPENSIVE home, every feature being studied for good effect. Cellar under entire house, with stone foundation. Steam heat is used. This house was erected in brick veneer at a cost of about $3,500 in plain finish for inside, and common good brick for exterior walls. The price can be varied of course, and when desired the plans can be prepared for a frame building without extra charge. Total width 40 feet 8 inches; the stories are 10 feet and 9 feet, cellar 7 feet.

It will be seen that there are no special features about this building to cost, beyond actual necessities, at the same time it has excellent proportions with great convenience, the essentials of a complete home.

DESIGN No. 13. **SQUARE HOUSE IN BRICK OR BRICK VENEER—(COLONIAL)** *Geo. F. Barber & Co., Arcts.*

COST, $3,800 TO $4,200

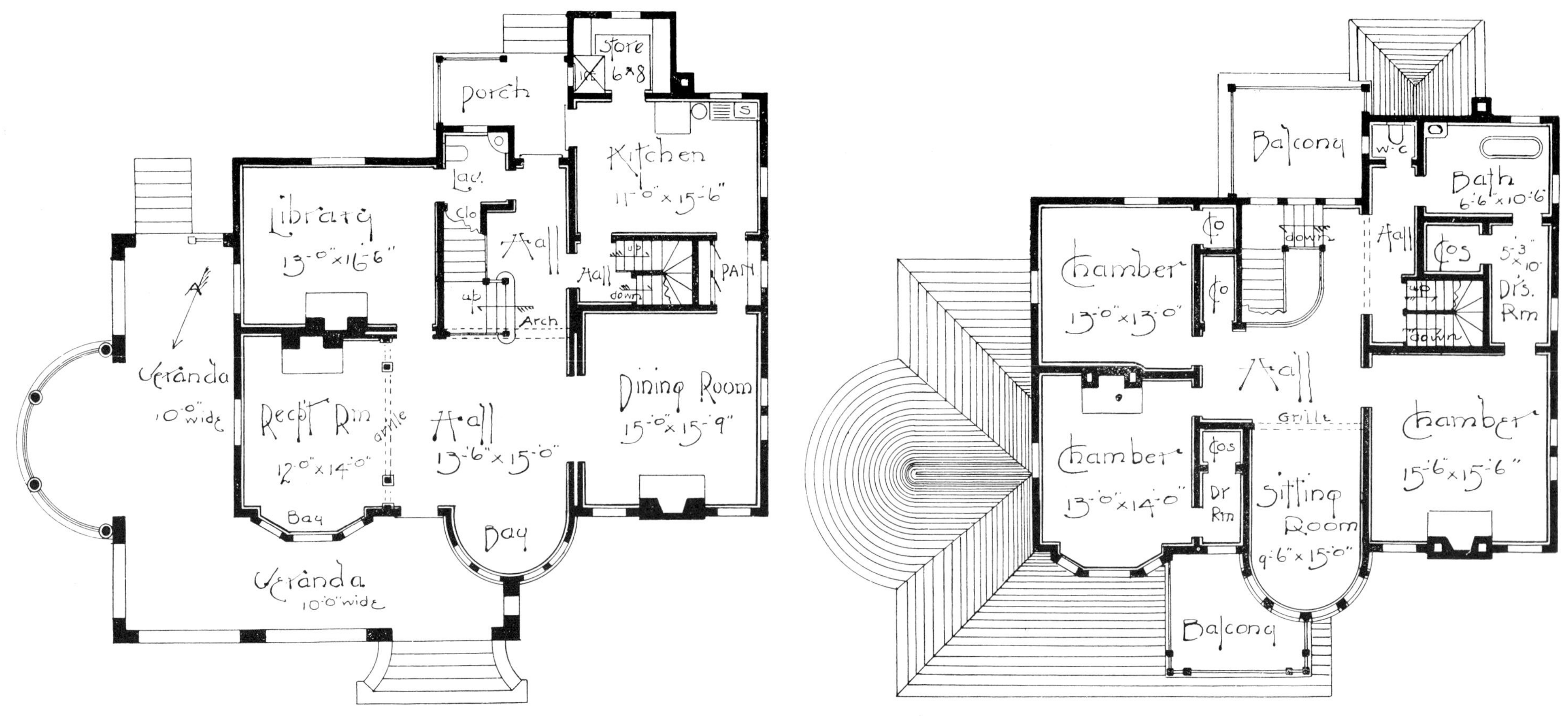

FLOOR PLANS FOR DESIGN No. 14

THIS is a home of which the owner is justly proud, and to which he has given the name of "**Pine Crest.**" The porch is an elegant feature of this house. The view of the furnished porch shown on page 38 is taken at A, viewed in the direction of the arrow. The main hall, divided from the reception-room by an artistic grille, is beautiful indeed, and the stairs, while plainly in view, are recessed enough to be entirely out of the main hall. Back of the hall, the library; to the right the dining-room, with a mantel and grate in front, ornamented by an art glass window in the chimney above the mantel. Every convenience possible has been arranged.

The style has been selected as a simple and plain rendering of Colonial for picturesque effect. Width over porches, 61 feet. Stories 10 feet and 9 feet 2 inches, respectively. Built in frame. Steam heat. Hardwood finish below, natural pine above.

We have recently furnished the plans in a cheaper form by making the tower octagon, leaving off the circle on the porch, placing a bath-room on the first floor in place of second floor near where the lavatory is now located. The cost of this house in the changed form was close to $2,500. One-fourth inch scale copies of these plans will be sent on application.

DESIGN No. 14. "PINE CREST"—COLONIAL RESIDENCE OF W. T. LANG, ESQ., KNOXVILLE, TENN. Geo. F. Barber & Co., Arcts

COST $4,000 TO $5,500

DESIGN No. 14. "PINE CREST" *Geo. F. Barber & Co., Arcts.*

VIEW SHOWING STAIRCASE FROM FRONT DOOR---DINING-ROOM AT RIGHT LIBRARY AT LEFT

DESIGN No. 14. **"PINE CREST"** *Geo. F. Barber & Co., Arcts.*

VIEW OF RECEPTION-ROOM FROM HALL---LIBRARY AT RIGHT

DESIGN No. 14. "PINE CREST"

VIEW OF HOUSE FROM SOUTHEAST

FRONT PORCH; *Geo. F. Barber & Co., Arcts.*

FROM POINT "A" ON THE FLOOR PLAN, SHOWING HOW ELEGANTLY IT MAY BE FURNISHED FOR AN AFTERNOON OR EVENING RECEPTION BY SIMPLY TRANSFERRING A FEW ARTICLES FROM THE INTERIOR

CORNER IN ONE OF OUR MISSISSIPPI HOMES

DESIGN No. 14. "PINE CREST" *Geo. F. Barber & Co., Arcts.*

VIEW IN HALL LOOKING TOWARD THE CIRCLE BAY FROM THE STAIRCASE

CORNER IN ONE OF OUR LOUISIANA HOMES

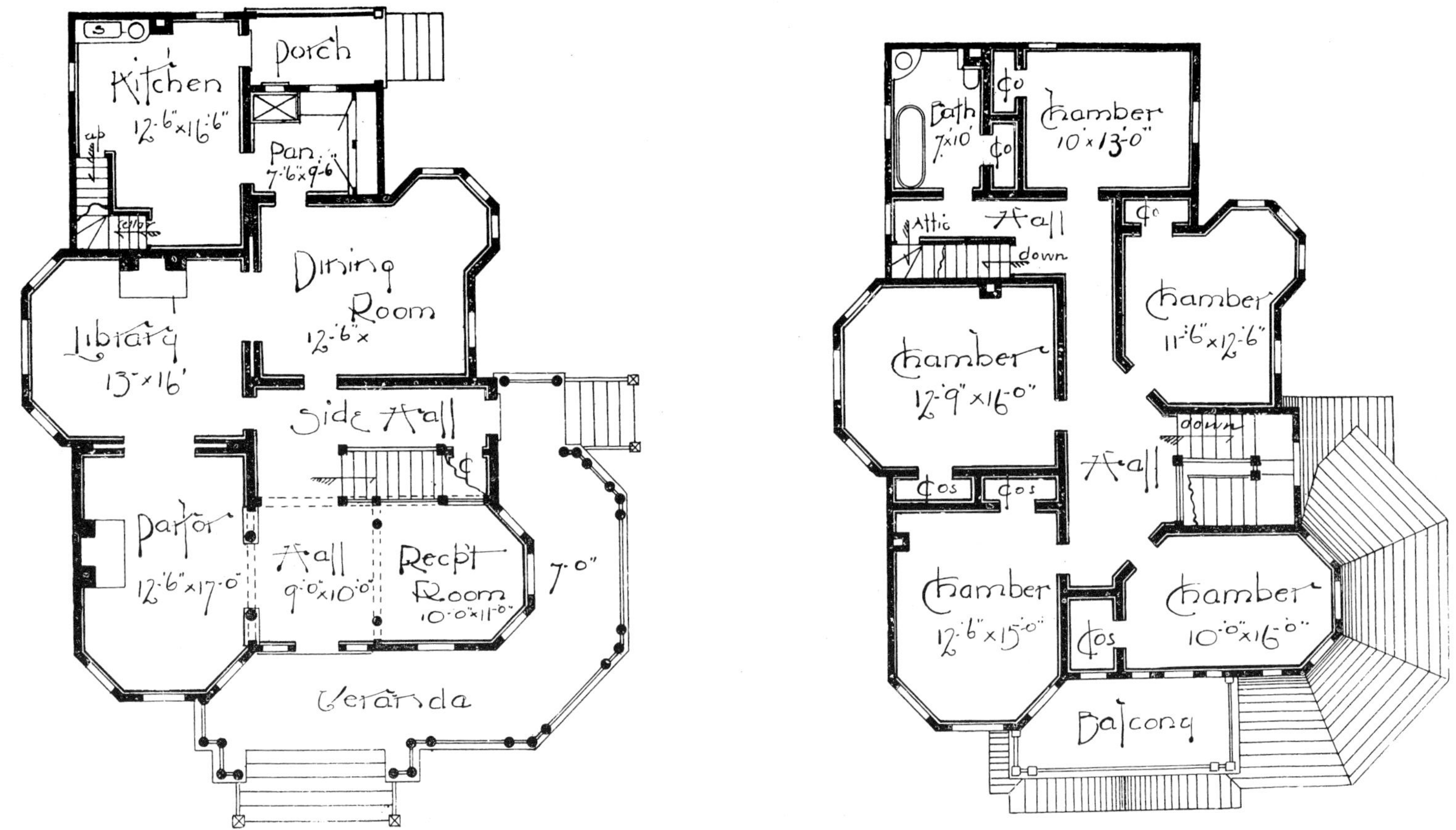

FLOOR PLANS FOR DESIGN No. 15

In this design we have a still different, yet handsome adaptation of Colonial treatment, many features having been employed to make it attractive from every point of view. This plan is superb. There is a front and side entrance to the hall from the porch. The hall has a beautiful and novel treatment of grille work, dividing stairs, reception-room and hall in a most fascinating manner. The exterior is shingled above the first story, including the roof. Cellar under main part, with provisions for steam-heating plant. The interior finish is hardwood for the main rooms, first floor, balance in natural pine. Size, 45 x 52 feet over porches. Stories, 10 feet and 9 feet 2 inches.

The dining-room is 12 feet 6 inches x 16 feet, and is augmented both in size and beauty by a deep bay built at such an angle as to make the outlook very pleasant indeed.

The refrigerator can be iced from the back porch, a convenience made possible by recent inventions. This, as all other designs in this book, are figured to be complete in all modern improvements.

DESIGN No. 15. A MODEL HOME—(COLONIAL) *Geo. F. Barber & Co., Arcts.*

COST $4,200 TO $4,700

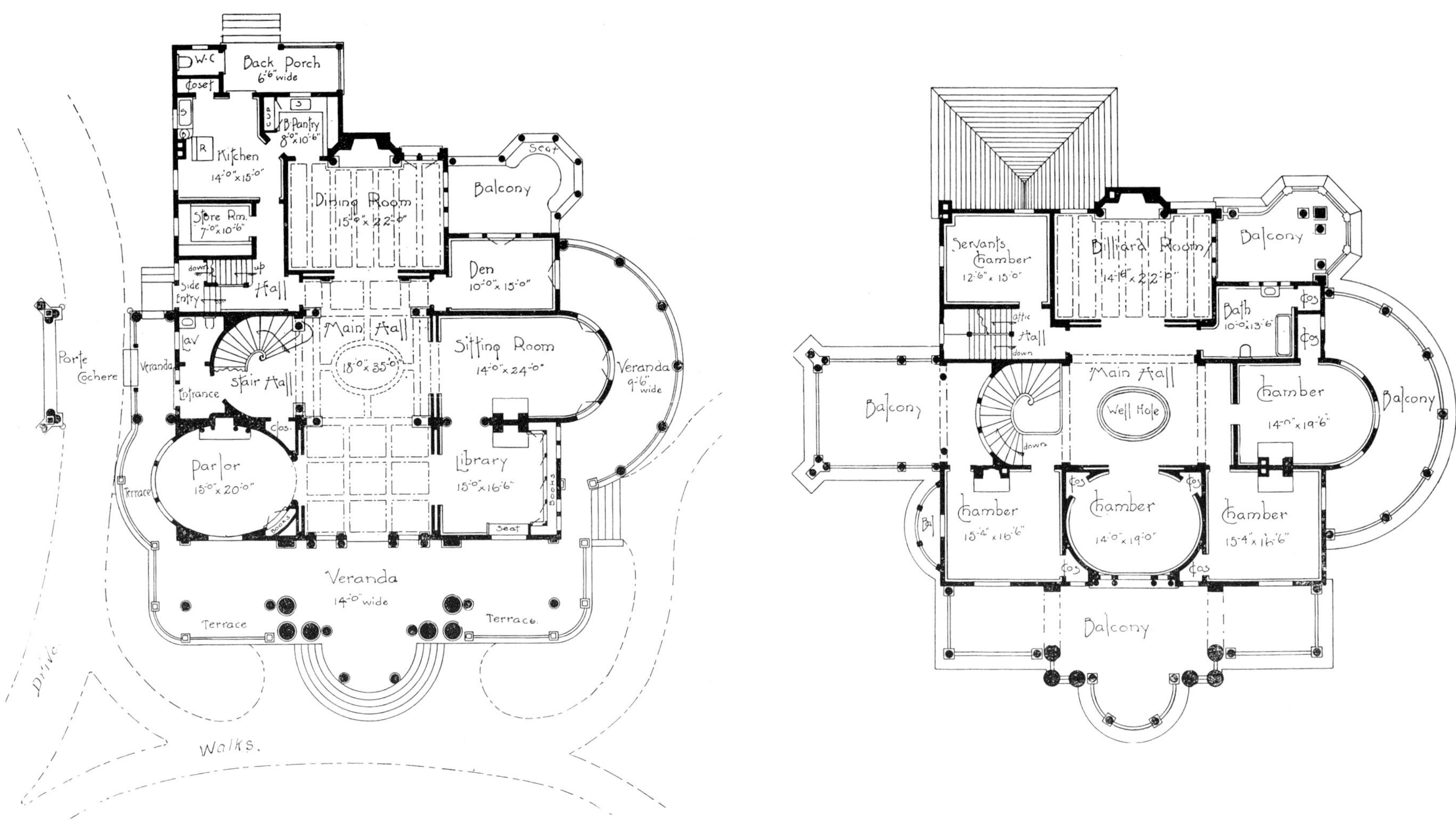

FLOOR PLANS FOR DESIGN No. 16

ONE SCARCELY ever sees a more elegantly arranged plan than the one here shown. On the front of the porch, first floor, we have carried the floor forward beyond the columns in a terrace for the reception and display of pot plants, which may be permanent or only as decorations on occasions of entertainments. These terraces are continued around and connect the side porches with the front.

Imagine a view from the front door through a handsomely columned and paneled hall to the dining-room, and its massive, specially designed Colonial mantel at the extremity of the view, and all other rooms to the right and left as handsomely, yet differently finished. When properly decorated and draped this home becomes a palace of elegance and comfort. A representative home for our many progressive American citizens. Complete in every modern appointment. Stories are 11 and 10 feet, respectively. Basement 8 feet. Attic finished as required.

Further information will be cheerfully given on application.

DESIGN No. 16. A BEAUTIFUL RENDERING OF MODERN GEORGIAN ARCHITECTURE—(CLASSIC COLONIAL) *Geo. F. Barber & Co., Arcts.*

COST, (ELEGANTLY FINISHED) $20,000 TO $25,000

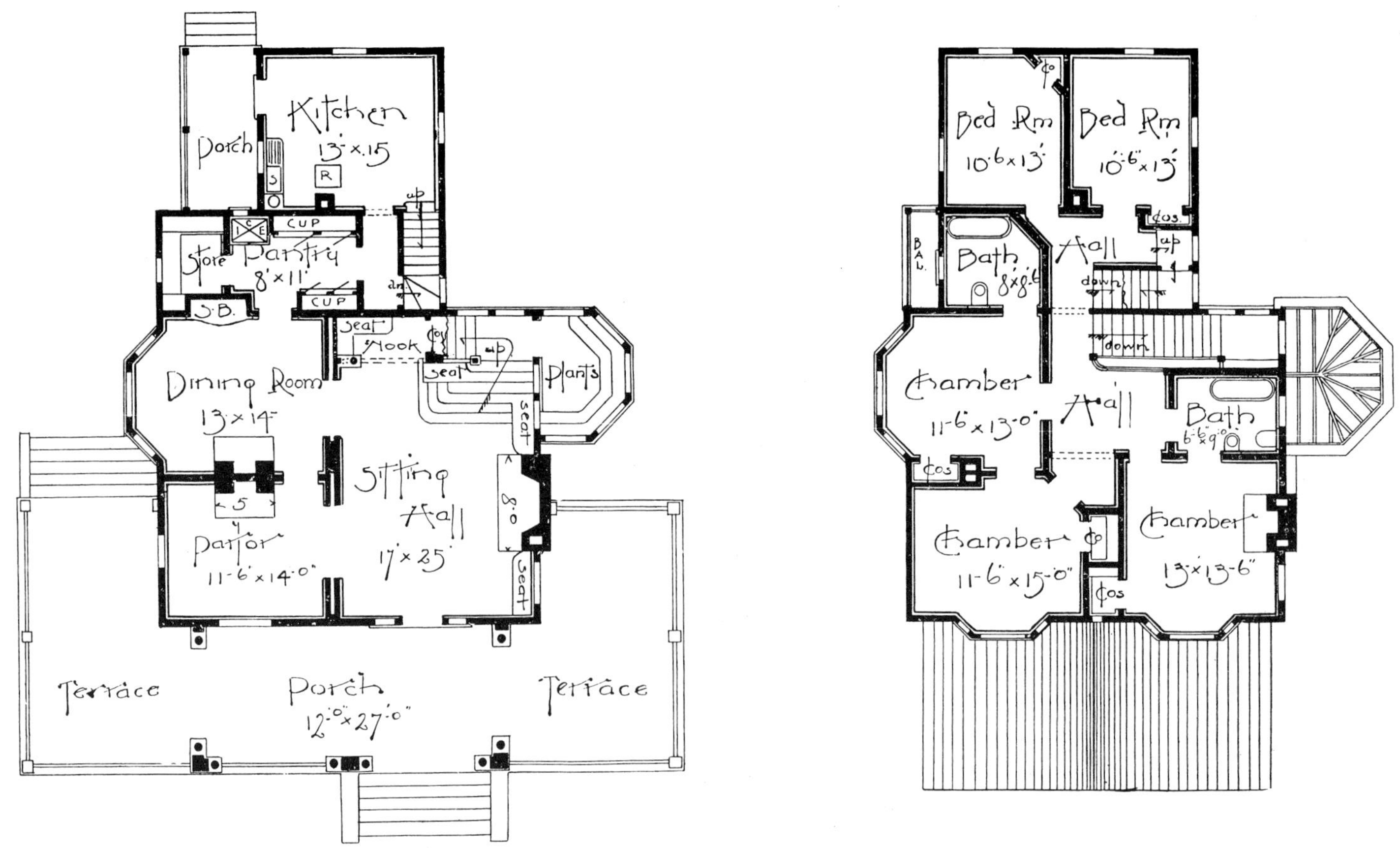

FLOOR PLANS FOR DESIGN No. 17

It is almost impossible to point out the many desirable features of this Maryland home. The hall, a very large room with a unique treatment of stairs from the landing of which one enters the conservatory. Two of the steps of the first flight widen out into convenient seats, while under the stairs we find place for a cosy nook with seat, and closet for coats, ornamented by an art grille. The broad 8-foot fireplace, either of brick, stone or wood, lends cheer on chilly days by its crackling flames. The kitchen is well away from the dining-room. The refrigerator is so located as to be iced from the porch. Five chambers and two bath-rooms, closets, etc., constitute a perfect second floor.

The 12 x 27 foot porch, flanked by large terraces, are pleasing features of the front. Size of house is, width 57 feet, length 60 feet. Stories 11 feet 6 inches and 9 feet 6 inches, respectively. Basement, 7 feet. Stone foundation. Roof and entire side walls from ground up shingled. A home complete in all modern requirements.

DESIGN No. 17. A CHOICE HOME IN DELIGHTFUL MARYLAND—(COLONIAL) *Geo. F. Barber & Co., Arcts.*

COST, $4,200 TO $4,500

INTERIOR OF HALL OF DESIGN No. 17

SHOWING STAIRCASE, NOOK UNDER IT AND ENTRANCE TO CONSERVATORY

INTERIOR VIEWS OF DESIGN No. 18

LOOKING FROM RECEPTION-ROOM THROUGH COLUMNED OPENINGS INTO PARLOR AND HALL

VIEW IN HALL, SHOWING STAIRCASE AND INTO DINING-ROOM---ALL FINISHED IN ENGLISH OAK

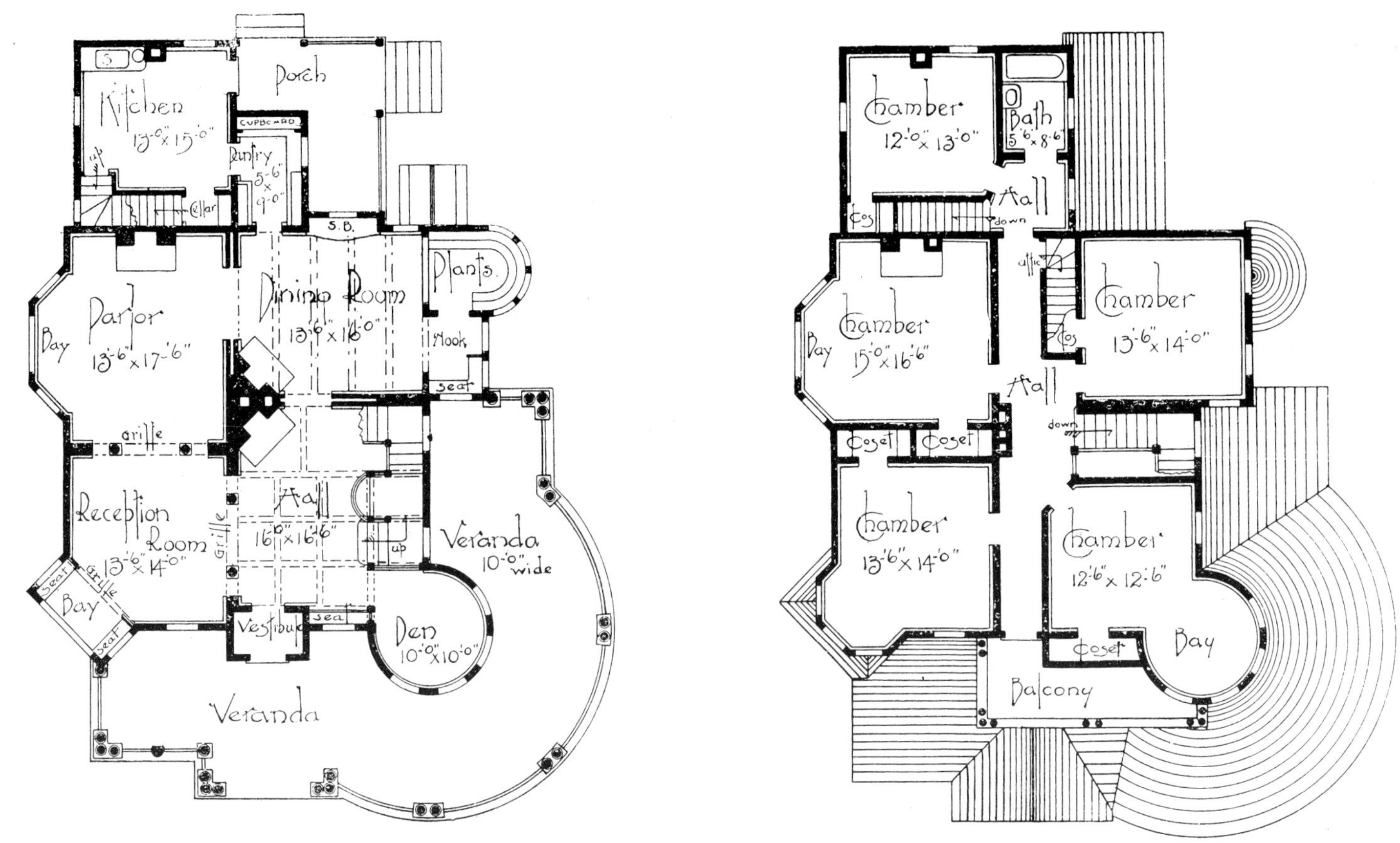

FLOOR PLANS FOR DESIGN No. 18

THIS artistic home is the residence of Mr. L. Terwilliger, New York City. Office under Fifth Avenue Hotel. Mr. Terwilliger, being a manufacturer of fine parquette floors and interior decorations, has had special designs prepared in his hall and other rooms for the elaborate use of these materials, the inside being largely finished in hardwood of choice kinds, and did not exceed $7,200.

A large cellar, stone foundation, with second story and roof shingled. Fine attic, and all throughout being first-class. It will be seen that the plan has many novel and beautiful features, and many good rooms.

The den is finished in Moorish with a grille of the same character cutting this room off from the hall. The same grille is carried from a full length stairpost across the stairs to the wall. The seat under the front window is only another part completing this finish. The dining-room nook is cut off by another grille of handsome design, and a large window gives a beautiful view of the conservatory.

Many handsome features are displayed everywhere in the shape of grilles, beams and columns, paneled ceilings, paneled wainscoting, parquette floors, etc., and is a complete home from every point of view.

DESIGN No. 18 **RESIDENCE AT RIDGEWOOD, N. J., HOME OF MR. L. TERWILLIGER, OF N. Y. CITY** *Geo. F. Barber & Co., Arcts.*

COST, $6,500 TO $7,200

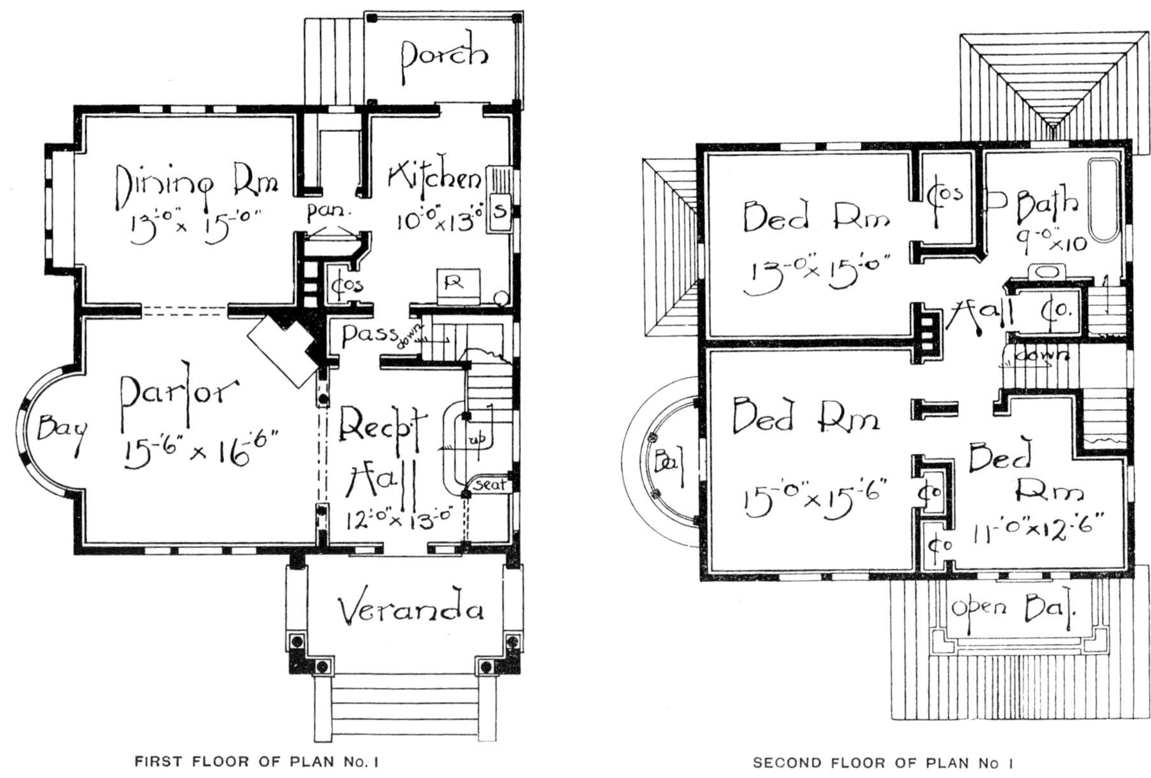

FIRST FLOOR OF PLAN No. I

SECOND FLOOR OF PLAN No I

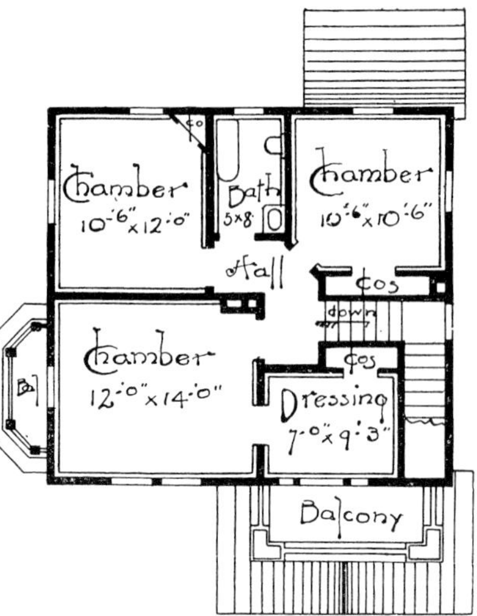

SECOND FLOOR OF PLAN No. 2

FLOOR PLANS FOR DESIGN No. 19

THIS ARTISTIC little Colonial home was recently erected from our plans by a lady in Colorado, at a very moderate price for so complete a plan, all of which were arranged from sketches submitted by the owner. A beautiful little home, complete in all modern requirements.

To the right, in the hall, the staircase is spanned by a handsome three-arched grille, and to the left the opening is supported by a heavy paneled beam and two artistic classic columns, and with all other features in strict keeping throughout the treatment is charming.

The exterior is a quaint but attractive rendering of Colonial. Height of first story is 9 feet 6 inches, second story 8 feet 6 inches. Dimensions 30 feet 6 inches wide by 37 feet in length.

In plan No. 2, we have this cottage reduced in size to cost from $1,800 to $2,000, arranged to be an attractive home in every particular.

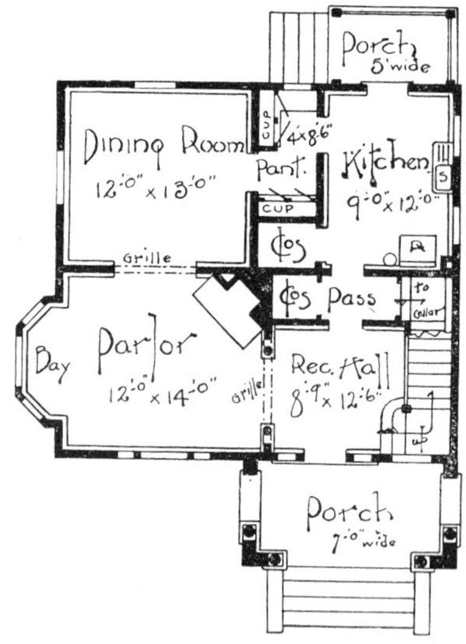

FIRST FLOOR OF PLAN No. 2

DESIGN No. 19. "COZY COT"—A HANDSOME COLONIAL HOME *Geo. F. Barber & Co., Arcts.*

COST, $2,500 TO $2,800

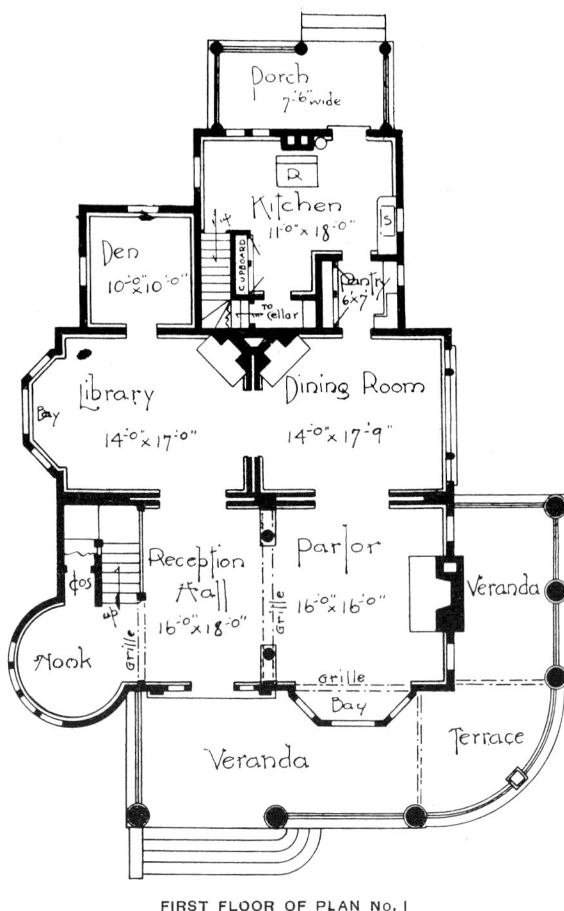

FIRST FLOOR OF PLAN No. 1

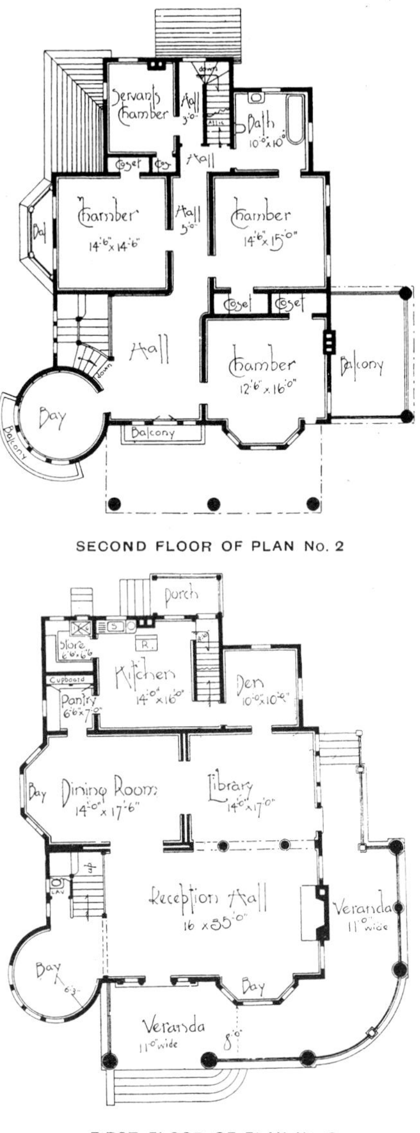

SECOND FLOOR OF PLAN No. 2

FIRST FLOOR OF PLAN No. 2

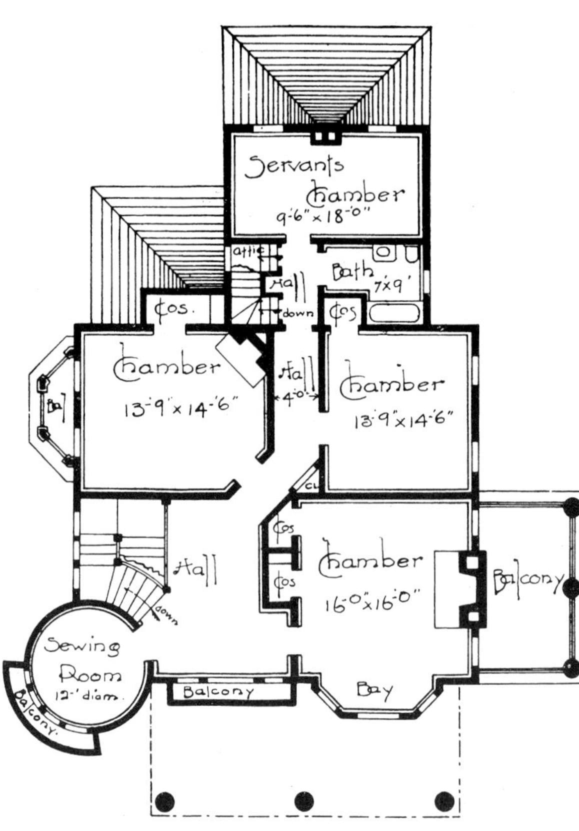

SECOND FLOOR OF PLAN No. 1

A HOME in the old-time Colonial style—a style that can be applied to almost any plan which will admit of the large stately columns and wide, heavy gables. The plan has a large hall extending across the entire front, part of it being termed the parlor. It is the hall simply divided by columns supporting a heavy Colonial beam at the ceiling, combining nicely with other rooms by a series of sliding doors. The cellar is under the entire house, with a low foundation of stone. The first story is finished in hardwood, with an elegant Colonial arched grille

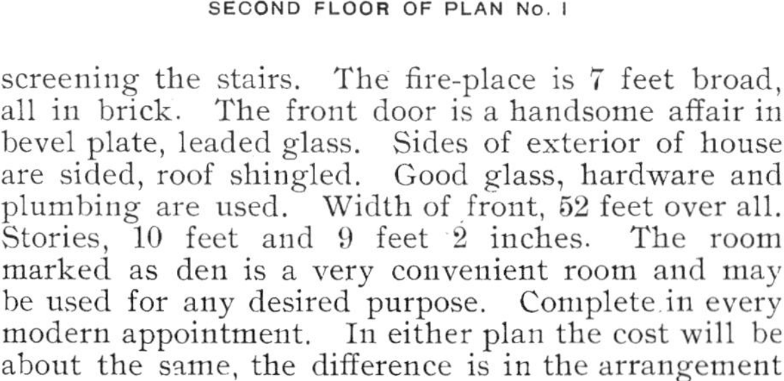

screening the stairs. The fire-place is 7 feet broad, all in brick. The front door is a handsome affair in bevel plate, leaded glass. Sides of exterior of house are sided, roof shingled. Good glass, hardware and plumbing are used. Width of front, 52 feet over all. Stories, 10 feet and 9 feet 2 inches. The room marked as den is a very convenient room and may be used for any desired purpose. Complete in every modern appointment. In either plan the cost will be about the same, the difference is in the arrangement —beautiful in both.

FLOOR PLANS FOR DESIGN No. 20

DESIGN No. 20. A POPULAR GEORGIAN HOME—(CLASSIC COLONIAL) *Geo. F. Barber & Co., Arcts.*

COST $4,500 TO $5,000

FLOOR PLANS FOR DESIGN No. 21

THE designs shown herewith illustrate a rather peculiar rendering of Colonial, but in good harmony of treatment. Ample and beautiful porticoes or porches are provided on all four sides in a well balanced manner, connected by terraces extending almost entirely around the house. The treatment of the porte-cochère is unique, and the rooms are elegant, making a convenient and commodious home.

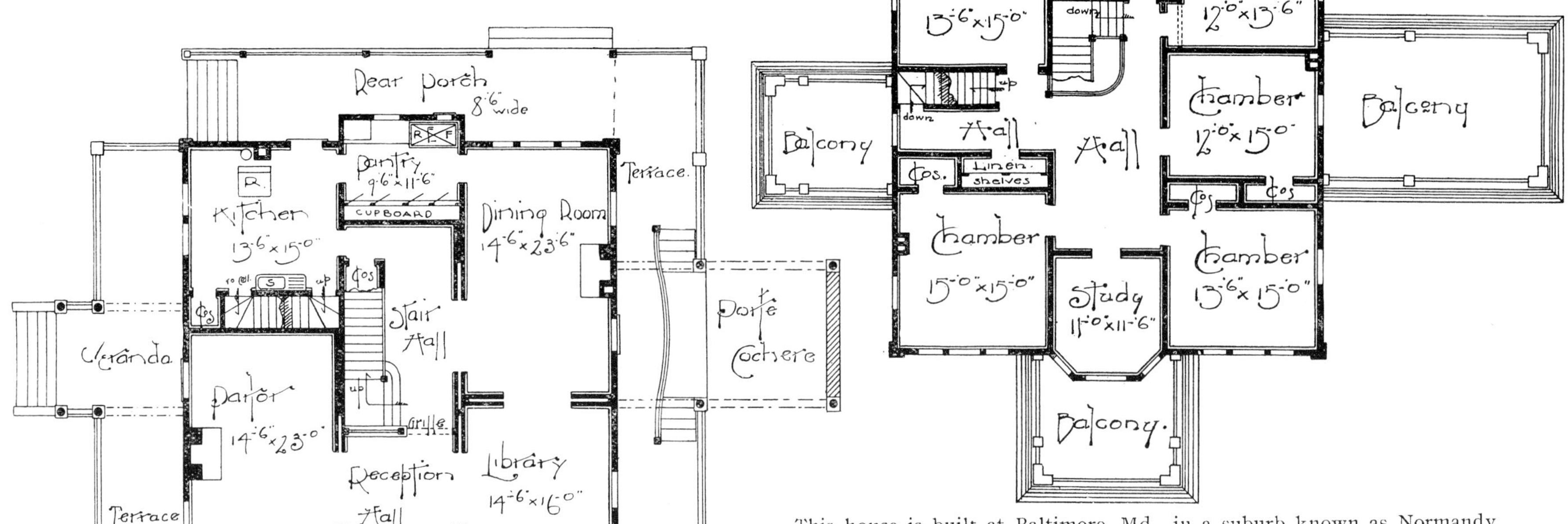

This house is built at Baltimore, Md., in a suburb known as Normandy Heights. This is one of forty-seven sets of plans we furnished to one party in Baltimore, eight of which were built at Normandy Heights. Three of the others are shown on pages 57, 59 and 61.

The price of this building includes a cellar under all and a finished attic. A private bath may be had on second floor by changing places with closet and linen-room, making the room a little wider. A lavatory under the front stairs in rear of hall would be desirable. Width of house 65 feet over porches only. Stories, 10 feet and 9 feet 2 inches. Cellar, 7 feet.

Complete in every modern appointment.

DESIGN No. 21. HANDSOME HOME AT NORMANDY HEIGHTS, BALTIMORE, MD.—(COLONIAL) *Geo. F. Barber & Co., Arcts.*

COST, $6,400 TO $6,800

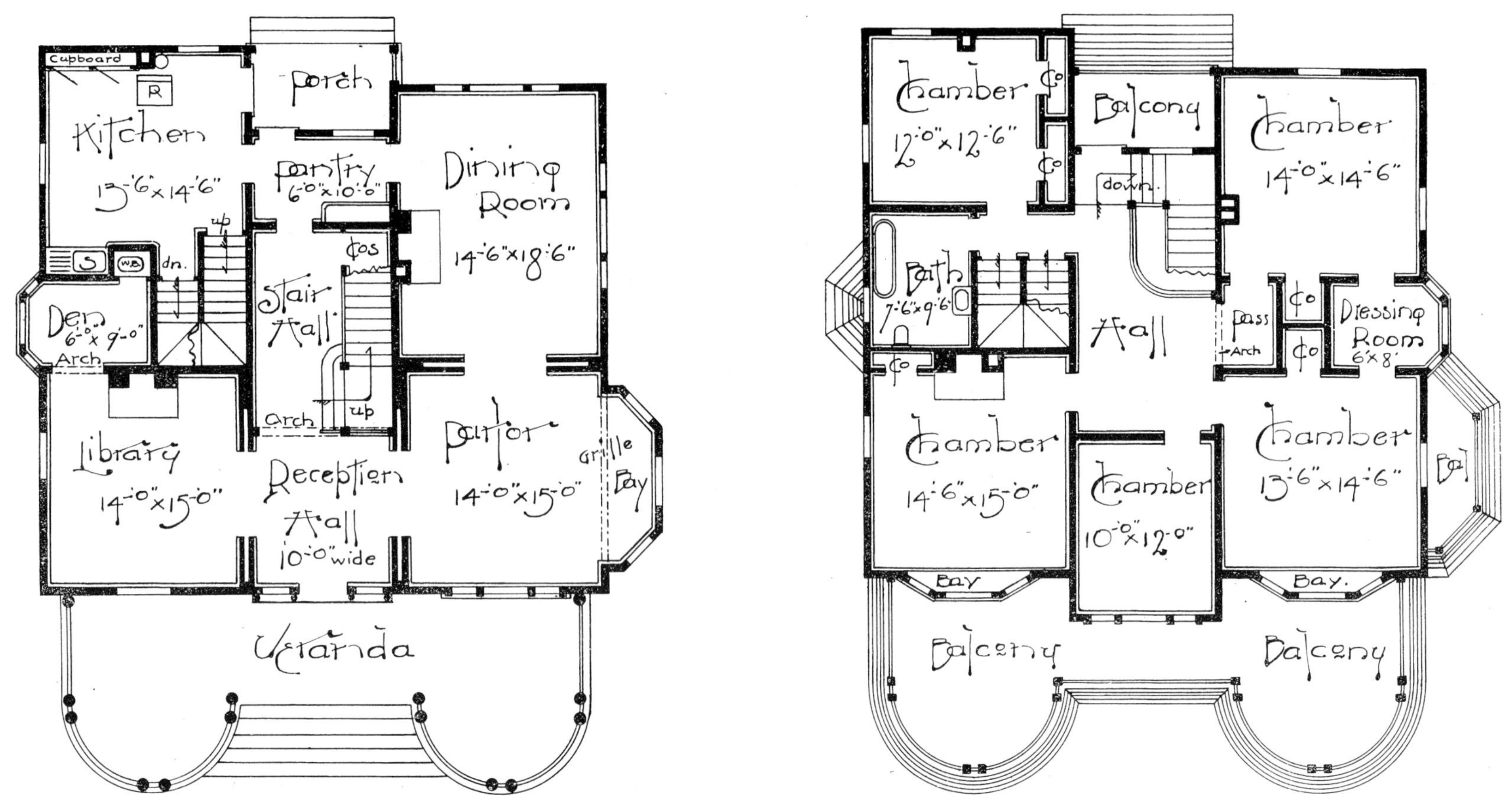

FLOOR PLANS FOR DESIGN No. 22

A MODEST but beautiful Colonial home. A porch of splendid design, gives finish to the front, from which one enters the reception hall, back of which an easy staircase is screened by a beautiful wood grille. The den off from the library will be appreciated by every user of the filthy weed. With this in view, a convenient washbowl is provided for this room.

A beautiful arrangement will be found throughout on both floors. Stories are 10 and 9 feet. Cellar 7 feet. Width over bay 45 feet. Fitted throughout in all modern appointments.

DESIGN No. 22. RESIDENCE AT NORMANDY HEIGHTS, MD.—(COLONIAL) *Geo. F. Barber & Co., Arcts.*

COST, \$5,200 TO \$5,700

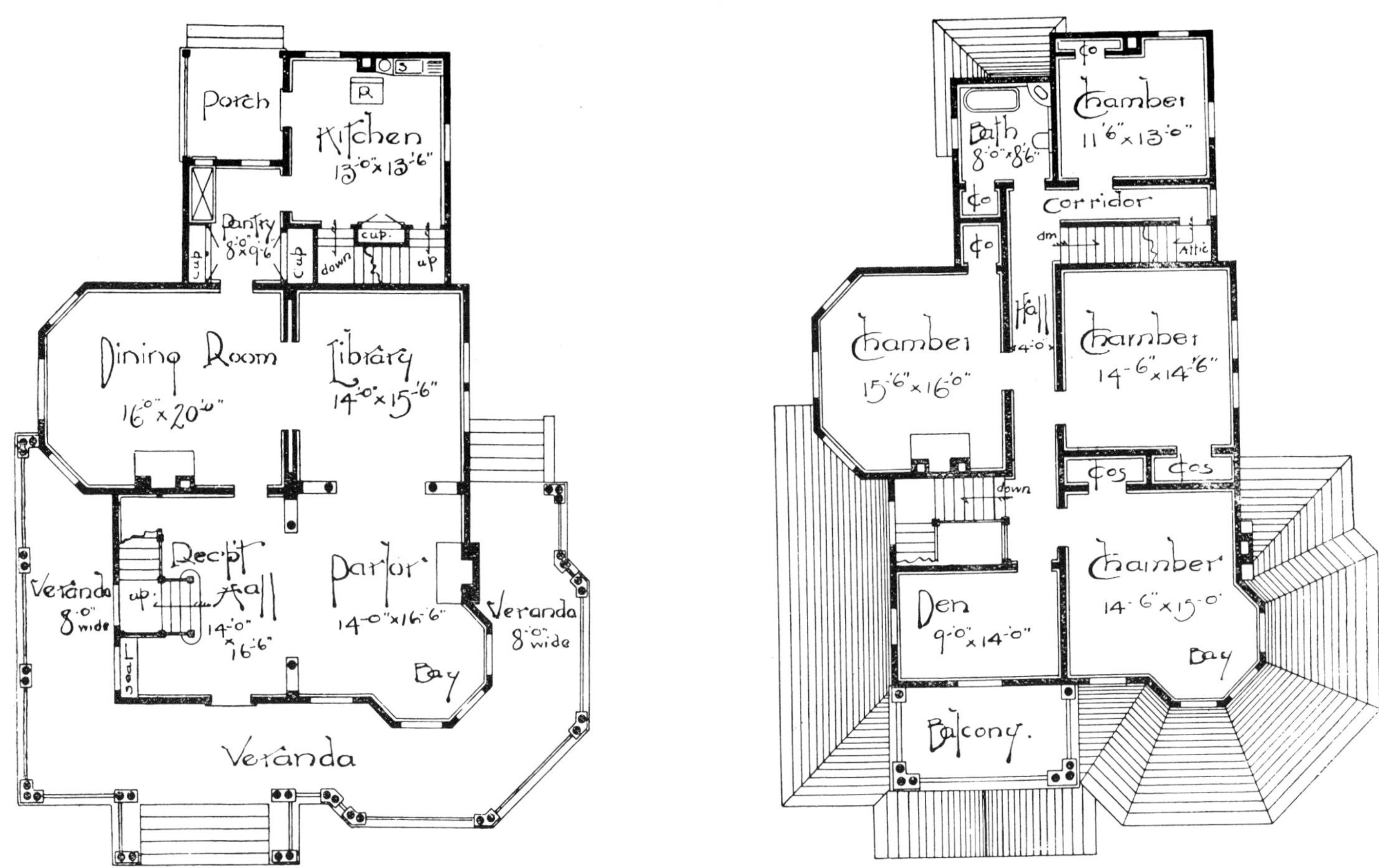

FLOOR PLANS FOR DESIGN No. 23

A HOUSE thrown wide open from hall to dining-room by the use of beamed and columned openings and sliding doors. A plain, though substantial house with a large, but appropriate, front balcony, a handsome tower and many attractive features. Has hardwood finish in the principal rooms. A good 7-foot cellar for heater, etc. The wide and extensive porch is a very desirable feature.

The stories are 10 feet and 9 feet 2 inches. Width of front over porches is 46 feet. A very desirable home indeed.

DESIGN No. 23. RESIDENCE AT NORMANDY HEIGHTS, MD.—(COLONIAL) *Geo F. Barber & Co., Arcts.*

COST, $5,500 TO $6,000

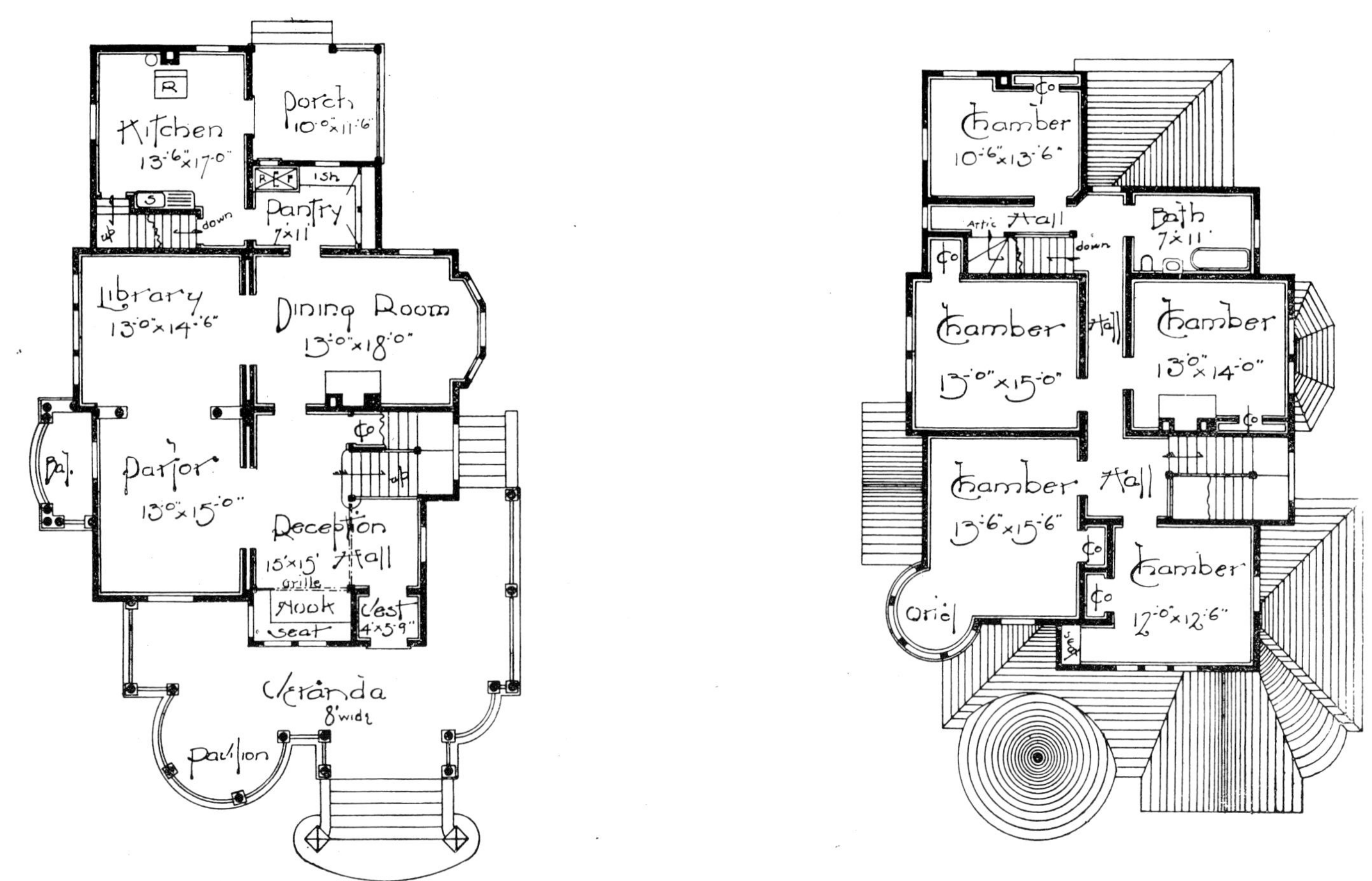

FLOOR PLANS FOR DESIGN No. 24

THE PLANS here given show a porch of special design, arranged for prominent and beautiful effect. The entire exterior is bold and striking. The hall vestibule is so placed as to give a good and ample entrance. Artistic wood grilles span the nook, and from the stairs to the vestibule a grille, partly draped with rich curtains, screens the main entrance a little.

The stories are 10 feet and 9 feet 2 inches, with cellar under main part 7 feet in the clear. Hardwood is liberally used for interior trimming on first floor. Good and complete finish throughout.

DESIGN No. 24. RESIDENCE AT NORMANDY HEIGHTS, MD.—(ROMANESQUE) *Geo. F. Barber & Co., Arcts.*

COST $6,500 TO $7,000

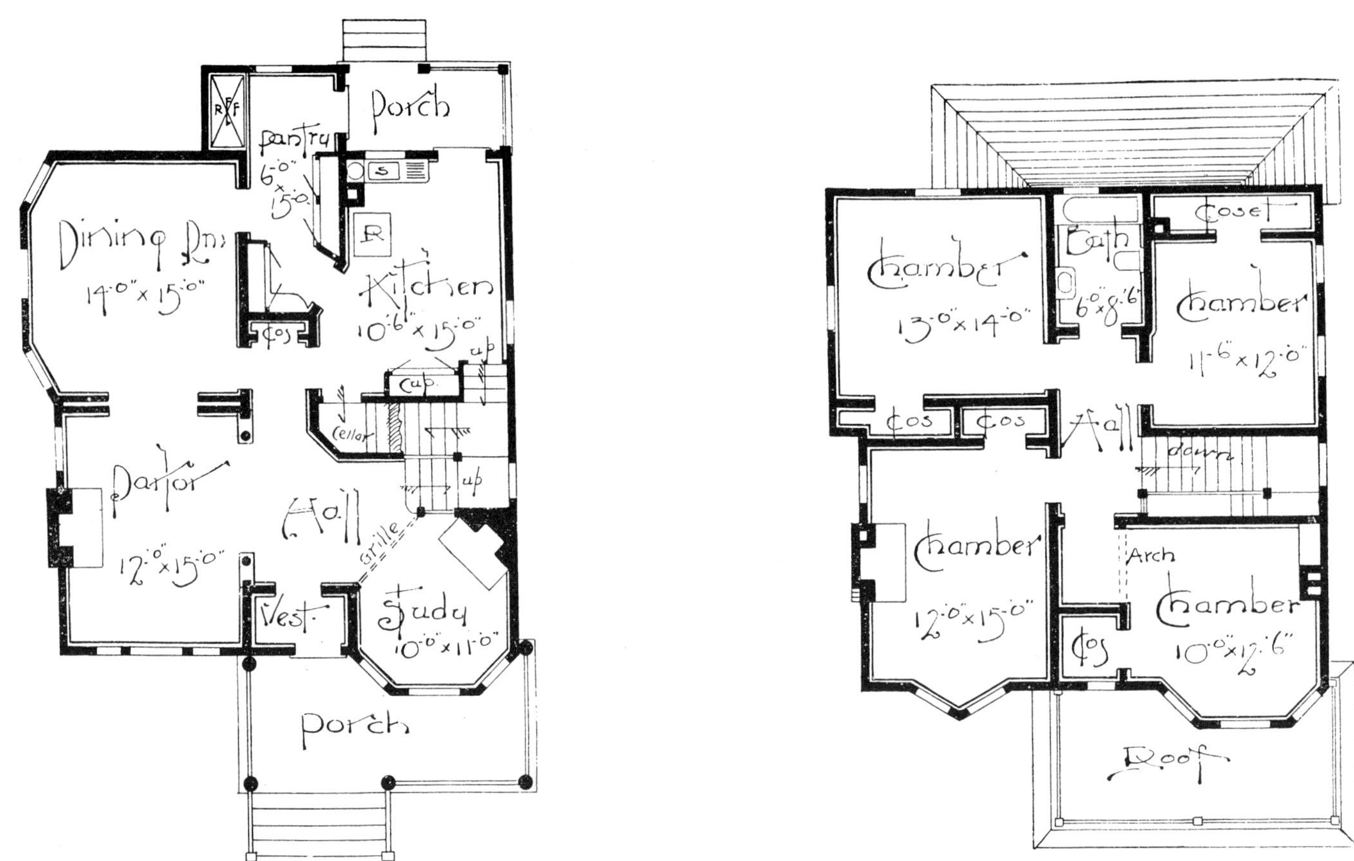

FLOOR PLANS FOR DESIGN No. 25

A MODEST but very handsome Colonial home. A design and plan arrangement that could scarcely be improved upon for so low a price. Suited to any locality or condition.

A magnificent hall, opening into all other rooms, and finished in three apartments in hardwood. The back and front stairs unite at the second landing. The pantry contains the refrigerator which can be reached from kitchen, dining-room and back porch, a great convenience. For the outside the second story and roof are shingled, the first story narrow weather-boarding. The cellar is 7 feet, under rear part. Foundation is stone. The stories are 10 feet and 9 feet 2 inches. Width of house is 30 feet 6 inches. The house is complete in all modern requirements.

DESIGN No. 25. **A TWENTIETH CENTURY HOME DESIGN—(COLONIAL)** *Geo. F. Barber & Co., Arcts.*

COST, $2,800 TO $3,200

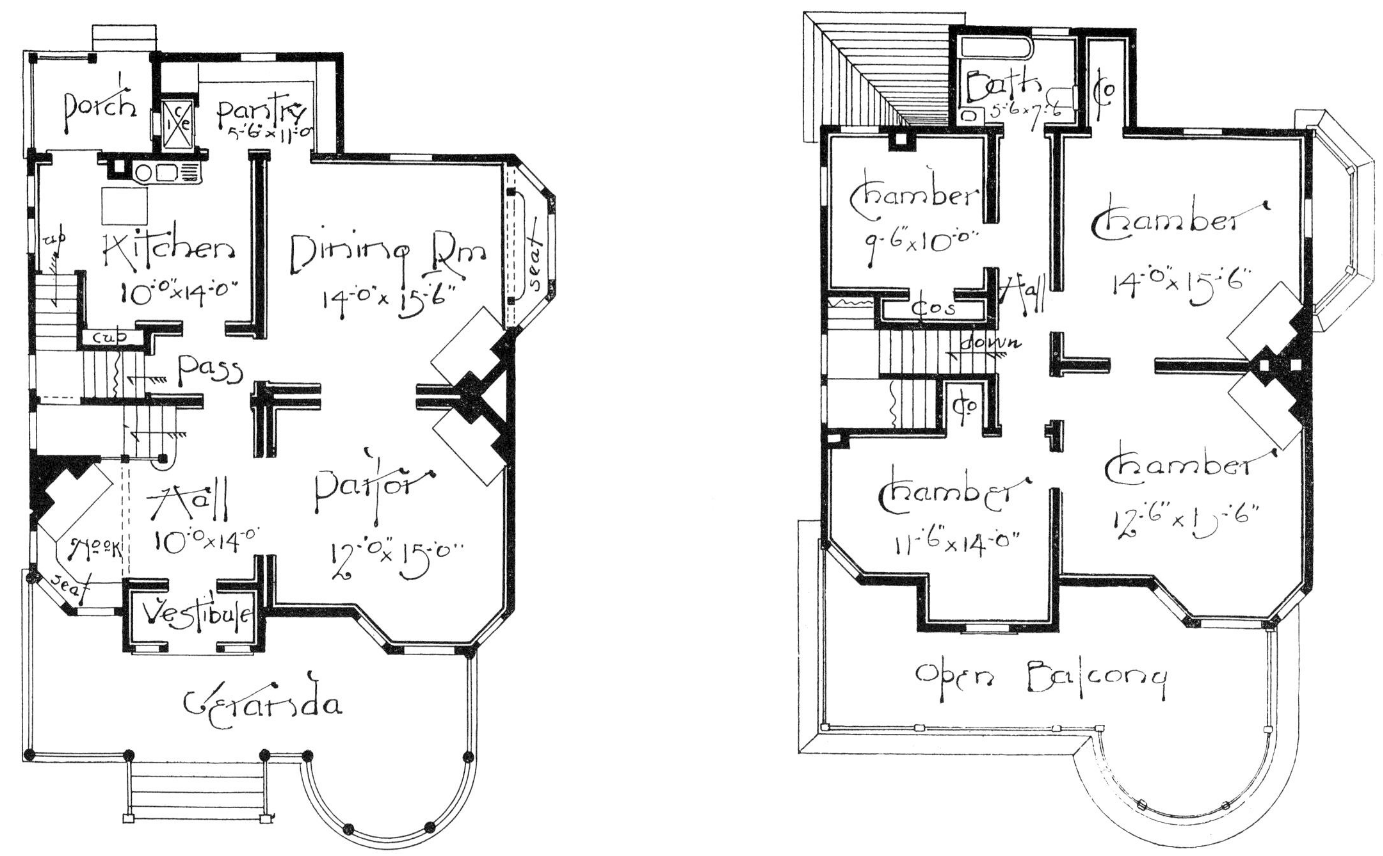

FLOOR PLANS FOR DESIGN No. 26

A HANDSOME, square, compact house, stripped of all unnecessary ornamentation. Contains one of the neatest halls imaginable. The parlor, dining-room, pantry, kitchen, back and front stairs are all excellent. A passage leads from hall to dining-room and kitchen, and to cellar way under stairs. All main rooms on both floors and hall below have fire-places.

A frame house, with second story and roof shingled. Cellar under back part only. The front door is of special and handsome design. The house is modernly equipped throughout. The ice-box is arranged in the pantry, with door for filling from the outside; it is thus away from the heat of the kitchen, yet convenient to both dining-room and kitchen. Width of front 34 feet. Stories are 10 feet and 9 feet 2 inches.

Correspondence cheerfully answered concerning any design shown in this book.

DESIGN No. 26. A HOME OF TWENTIETH CENTURY IDEAS—(COLONIAL) Geo. F. Barber & Co., Arcts.

COST, $2,800 TO $3,200

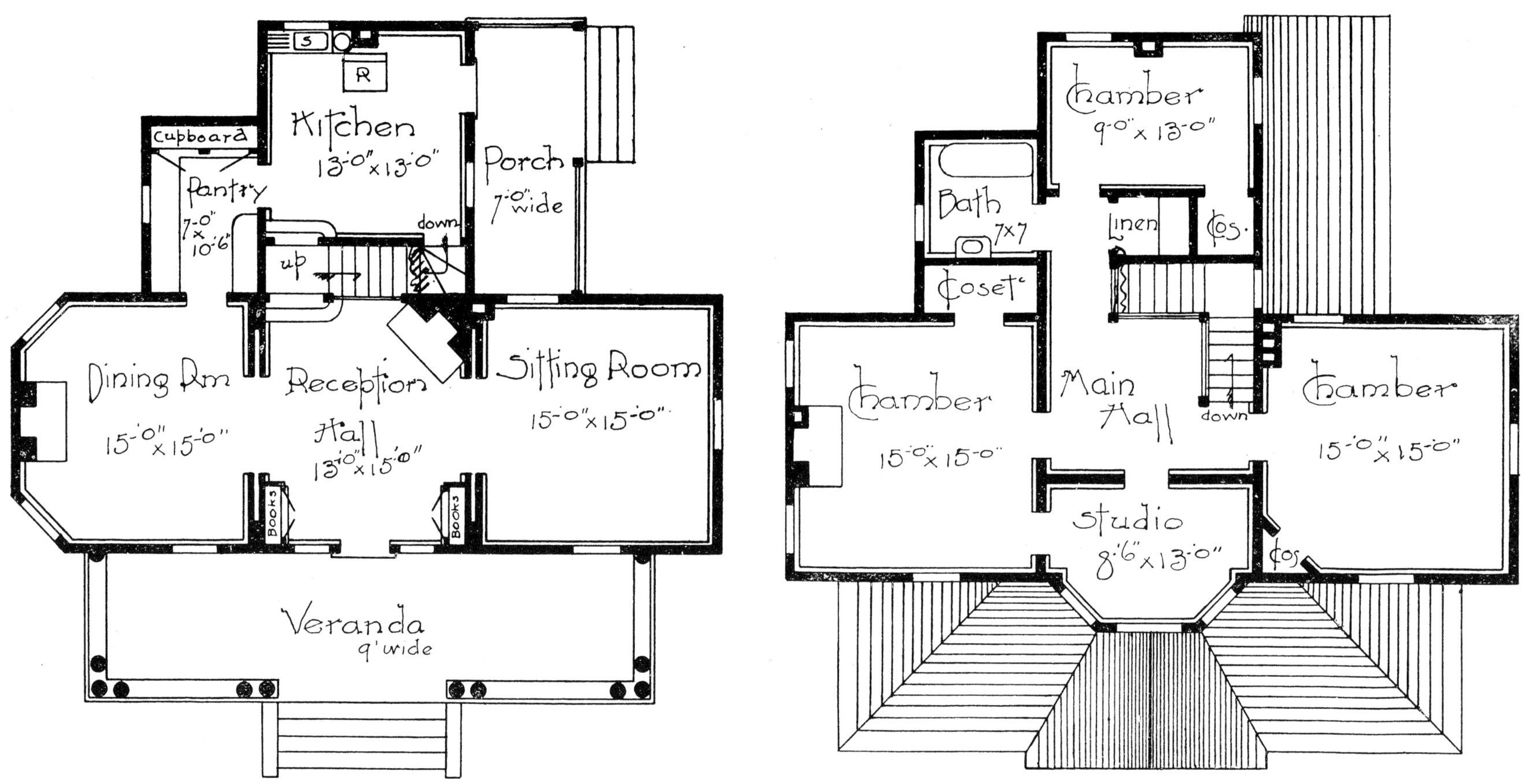

FLOOR PLANS FOR DESIGN No. 27

THIS is the home of the lady who so beautifully contributes to the *Woman's Home Companion* on decorative painting on china. The ideas to be carried out in planning this home were three rooms in front, one of them to be a reception hall of such size and proportions that it could be used also as library and sitting-room, using the sitting-room proper as a parlor, and, if need be, as a bed-room.

The interior views on page 69 show the neat appearance of two of these rooms. The cost of the house, finished largely in oak, was $2,800. The dimensions are: width 46 feet, length 42 feet, stories 10 and 9 feet.

DESIGN No. 27. RESIDENCE OF MRS. MARY MOSS CALDWELL, GLASGOW, KY. *Geo F. Barber & Co., Arcts.*

COST, $2,800

SUGGESTIONS IN PORCHES

MODERN in design, artistic in construction, showing suggestive pavilions, broad gables and steps, artistic grouping of columns, and other features worthy of study.

FURNISHED PORCH FOR DESIGN No. 27

A VIEW of the porch, residence of Mrs. M. M. Caldwell, as furnished for an afternoon chat with old friends and acquaintances, displaying the elegant taste of the owner, and giving an air of ease and home comfort.

INTERIORS. RESIDENCE OF MRS. M. M. CALDWELL, DESIGN No. 27

VIEW OF STAIRS AND MANTEL IN RECEPTION HALL

VIEW LOOKING FROM DINING-ROOM THROUGH HALL INTO SITTING-ROOM

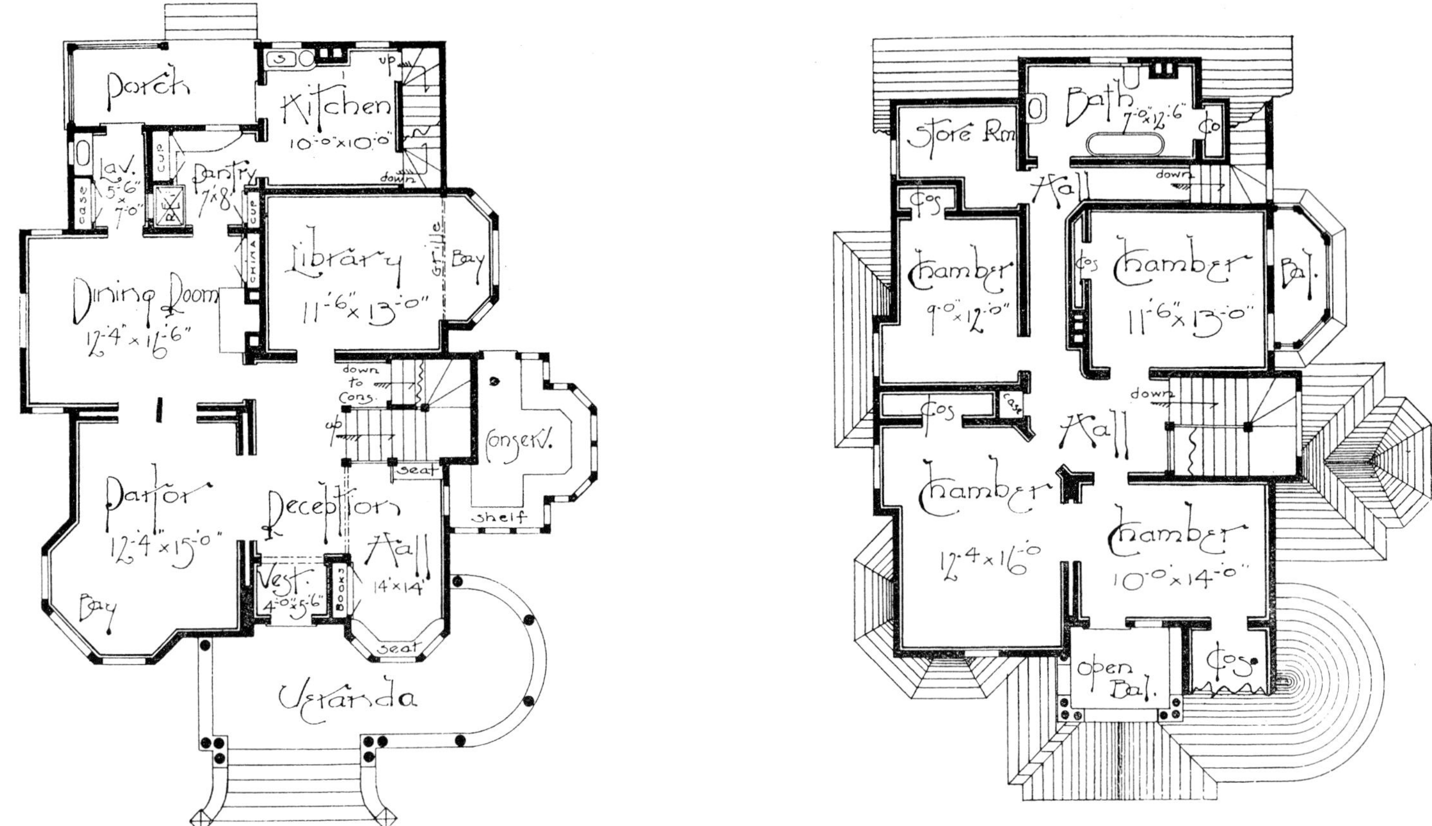

FLOOR PLANS FOR DESIGN No. 28

THIS house, though not so large, is elaborately finished in the choicest of hardwoods. The vestibule is in curly maple; hall in choice quartered white oak, the general features of which are shown on other pages; an elegant bookcase being built in near the bay; the grille is of oak, made by Geo. L. Thompson Co., of Chicago, and is very fine indeed. Under the stairs we descend to the conservatory, a view of which is had from the hall through the window.

The parlor is in white curly maple, and polished, smooth as plate-glass. The dining-room is in curly birch, shaded to a rich cherry color and polished. The library is in quartered sycamore. All the second floor is in natural Tennessee pine, a beautiful wood. A cellar is under the kitchen and library and contains a Furman steam boiler. The first floor is laid double with waterproof paper and a half-inch air space between. The exterior walls are sheathed and papered and paper is laid on the roof under the slate. One indirect radiator is placed in the floor of the hall. This brings in a constant current of hot, fresh air from the outside. Weather-boarding and cypress shingles are used on the outside walls.

There are many excellent features about this design that makes it a delightful home. The interior views shown on pages 72, 73 and 77 will give some idea of the interior finish and design.

DESIGN No. 28. RESIDENCE OF C. A. NICKERSON, ESQ., KNOXVILLE, TENN. *Geo. F. Barber & Co., Arcts.*

COST, $4,000 TO $4,200

INTERIOR OF HALL, RESIDENCE OF HON. CHURCH HOWE AUBURN, NEB. SEE PAGE 121

VIEW FROM VESTIBULE IN HALL OF DESIGN No. 28, SHOWING STAIRS AND GRILLE WORK

A CORNER IN THE PARLOR OF ONE OF OUR TEXAS HOMES FINISHED HANDSOMELY THROUGHOUT

VIEW SHOWING STAIRS AND GRILLE TREATMENT OF DESIGN No. 28---VIEW FROM THE PARLOR THROUGH THE SLIDING DOORS TO THE HALL

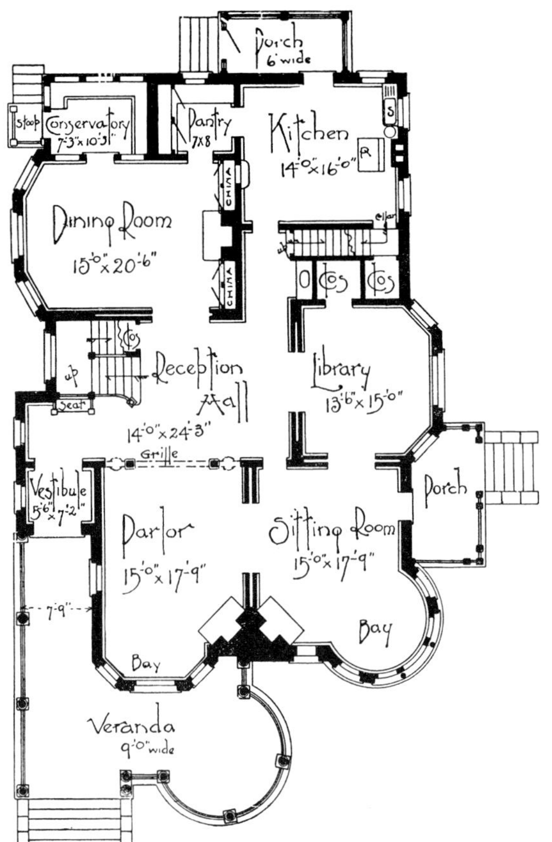

THE parties doing the interior decorating and furnishing of this house write us as follows:

"Replying to your favor of the 18th inst., we wish to say that the entire furnishing and decorating, including furniture made to order from special designs, also rugs and carpets, were included in our contract. This work has been handled in the Colonial style throughout, using mostly mahogany furniture. The parlor is treated in a Louis XVI. Colonial style, in apple-green. The carpet, draperies, laces, furniture and upholstering materials all were selected to harmonize with style of room in color and drawing. The sitting-room is more to the Louis XIV., in Rose Du Barry, treated with oriental rugs on floor. The dining-room is a tapestry room in blue.

Yours very truly,
HUNGATE & BOWMAN,
285 Erie St., Cleveland, Ohio."

The interior views on pages 76 and 77 will give an idea of the excellence of the interior design.

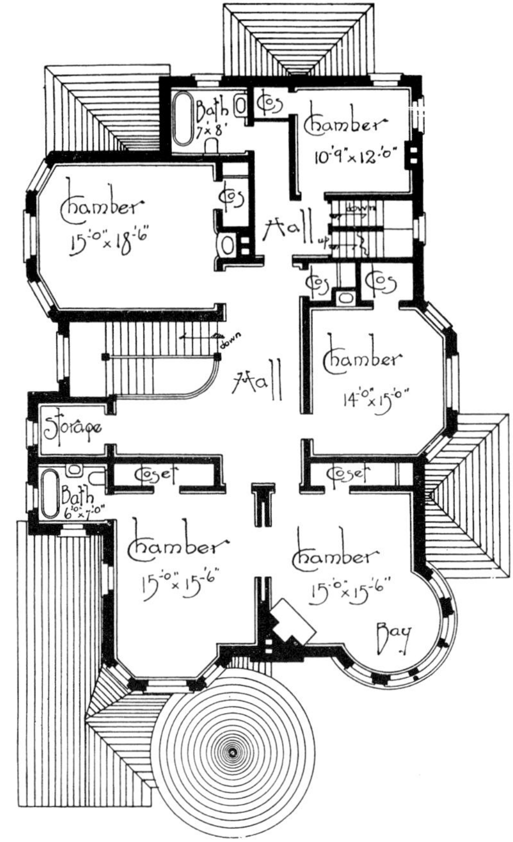

FLOOR PLANS FOR DESIGN No. 29

THE above design shows the new home of one of our clients at Keokuk, Ia. It represents an expenditure of some $12,500, in a combination of stone, brick and wood. A cellar is under the entire house. The foundation and first story are of rock-faced broken ashlar stones, buff in color; the second story in St. Louis white-coated brick, all being veneered on a wood frame, making the best house possible.

The roof is slated—all glass, hardware and plumbing being of nicest and best quality of their respective kinds, and the workmanship throughout is of the best. The Haxton steam boiler is used for heating, with American Radiator Co's. radiators, Rococo pattern. Quarter-sawed oak floors are in all rooms except parlor and one room upstairs.

The library, sitting-room, parlor, reception hall, vestibule and two front chambers are embellished with best American plate glass, which adds beautifully to the finished appearance of any home. The tower glass is bent to proper radius. The ceiling of the hall is paneled in quartered oak. Berry Brothers' varnish is used throughout.

Length 80 feet, over porches, width 48 feet. Stories 11 feet and 10 feet, respectively. The pavilion of the porch is 14 feet 6 inches in diameter. The inside diameter of the circular tower is 11 feet.

DESIGN No. 29. **A DELIGHTFUL HOME IN PROGRESSIVE IOWA** *Geo. F. Barber & Co., Arcts.*

COST, $12,500

VIEW OF GRILLE LOOKING FROM HALL INTO PARLOR IN RESIDENCE SHOWN IN DESIGN No. 29

THIS grille is of oak, patterned somewhat after the Moorish, and spans the entire space between the hall and parlor. On the paneled bases at the two sides semi-circular corbles, beautifully carved, support a circular top for support of pot plants, statuary and the like. The effect is always beautiful, and may be used in any house where the space is wide. The heavy beam and column treatment can be used in place of the grille, if preferred, using the Ionic style. On account of some special hand-carving this grille is quite expensive, but very rich.

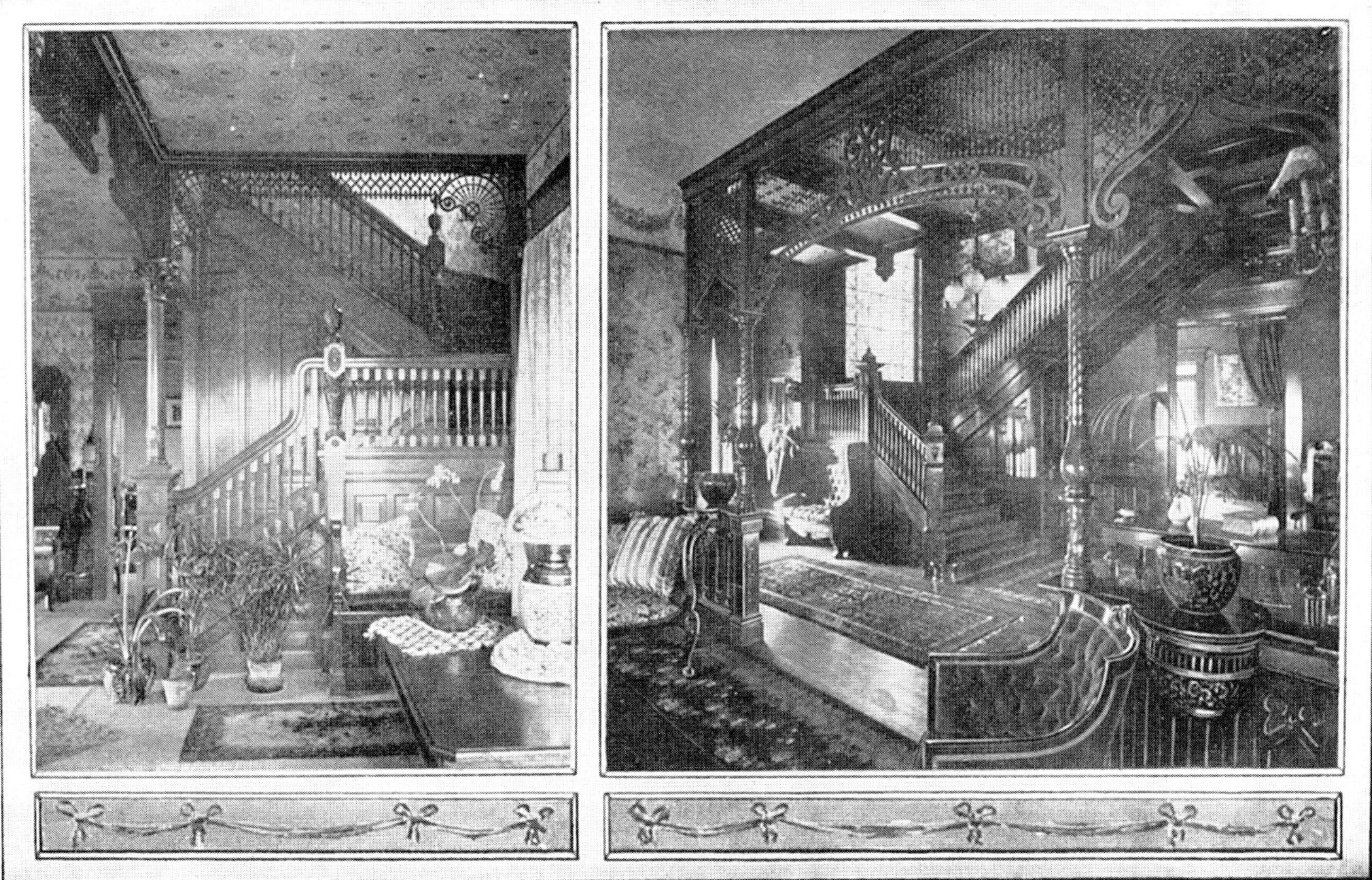

VIEW OF STAIRS AND GRILLE IN DESIGN No. 28

Showing the beautiful relations between the two as viewed from the hall nook. The three views of this interior are valuable studies.

ANOTHER VIEW OF HALL IN DESIGN No. 29

Looking from the parlor toward the staircase, showing the beautiful application of the grille and its elegant harmony with all other surroundings.

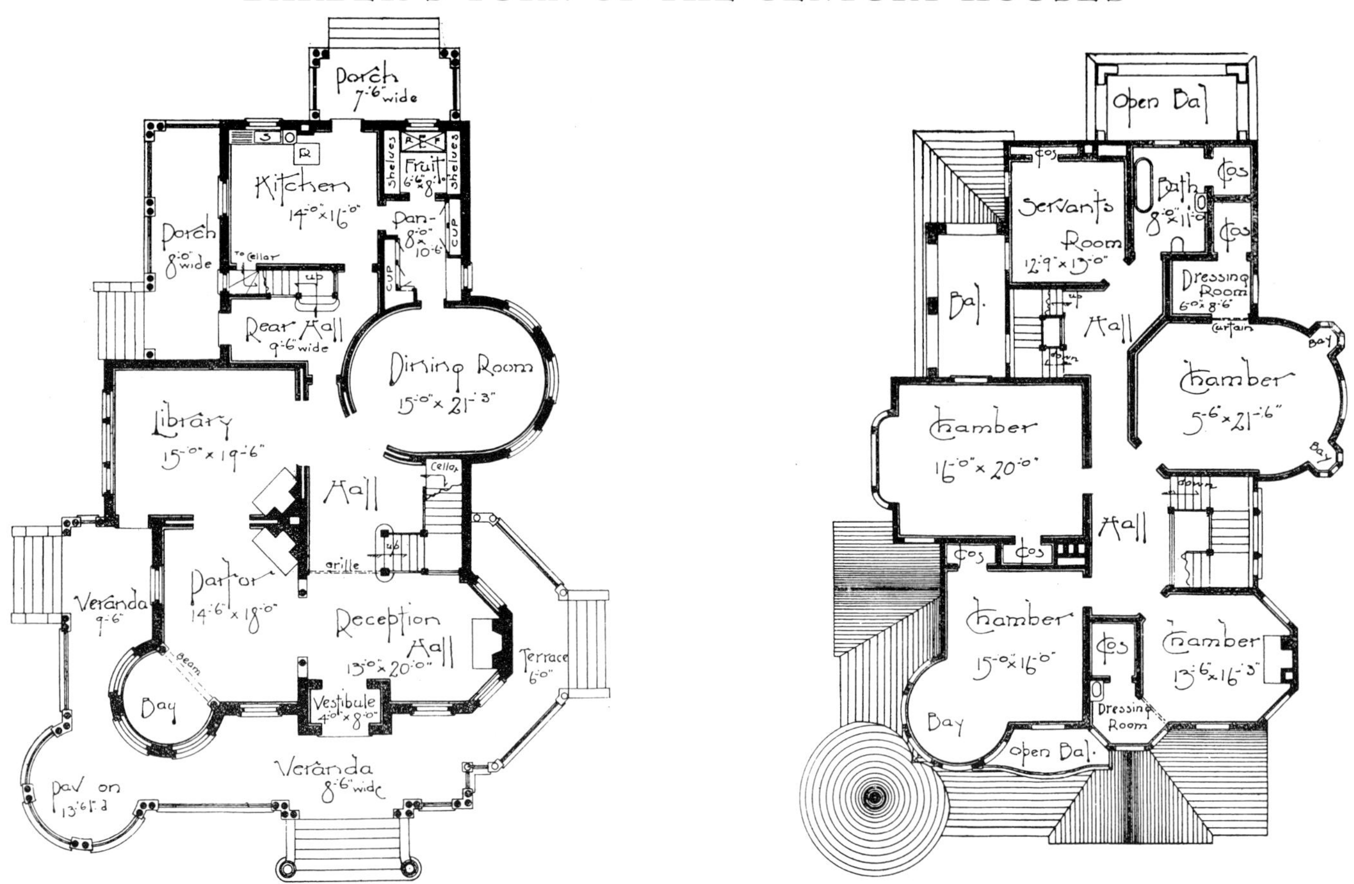

FLOOR PLANS FOR DESIGN No. 30

THESE PLANS call for a house of stately appearance, beautiful proportions in every feature, and is a house suitable for most any position or location. Finished complete, from cellar to garret, in the best of materials and workmanship. The dining-room is elliptical. The hall roomy and planned for beautiful treatment and embellishment.

The main roof, over the hall and dining-room, not shown in the cut, is treated in an artistic manner, and is a beautiful feature of the design. The roof is of slate, and with the finials and roof of tower in copper, the effect is beyond description. The first story is in brick veneer with shingles for the second story, though any materials may be used by paying difference in cost, if any. Length 70 feet 6 inches by 55 feet 6 inches in width, over porches. Stories 11 feet and 10 feet, respectively.

The house, as shown, is the residence of W. H. Baker of Winchester, Va. The same house, with slight changes, was erected for W. G. Newman of New York, as a summer residence on a hill near Somerset, Va., and may be seen from the train about two miles to the northeast of the village. It cost Mr. Newman some $40,000, but the walls are of Tennessee brown stone, broken ashlar. The porch columns are of Tennessee marble, polished, with Ionic caps carved from the same material. The roof is of red slate, and the finials on all towers are very elaborate, made of copper and gilded with pure gold leaf, and sparkle beautifully in the sunlight.

Interior views are shown on pages 80 and 81, and a view of the furnished pavilion is shown on page 82.

DESIGN No. 30.

RESIDENCE AT WINCHESTER, VA.

COST, $10,000 TO $12,000

Geo. F. Barber & Co., Arcts.

DESIGN No. 30. *Geo. F. Barber & Co., Arcts.*

INTERIOR VIEWS---FROM PHOTOGRAPHS

RIGHT PERSPECTIVE VIEW---FROM PHOTOGRAPH

ANOTHER VIEW IN MR. NELSON'S MURFREESBORO RESIDENCE

Showing the stairs in the hall. The plan below gives an idea of the treatment of the second landing with curved railing.

VIEW IN THE HALL IN RESIDENCE OF DESIGN No. 30

Showing stairs, grille, etc. See other views of this elegant home on pages 78, 79 and 80.

STAIR TOWER FILLED WITH ART GLASS FROM ONE OF OUR MISSISSIPPI HOUSES

THIS furnished spot of open air dwelling in the rotunda of the porch in Design No. 30 shows how elegantly we can furnish and arrange the pavilion of a porch.

A FRONT OUTLOOK FROM ONE OF OUR NORFOLK, VA., HOUSES

SUGGESTION for the treatment of a two-story porch or gallery, showing treatment of balcony and gable over the front steps, from one of our Mississippi homes.

VIEW showing a system of elegant draping on a large art window in the home of Mr. Jno. H. Nelson, of Murfreesboro, Tenn., erected from our plans.

ANOTHER view of two-story porch in a Mississippi residence, showing an elegant and appropriate method of treating the corner of the porch with a pavilion.

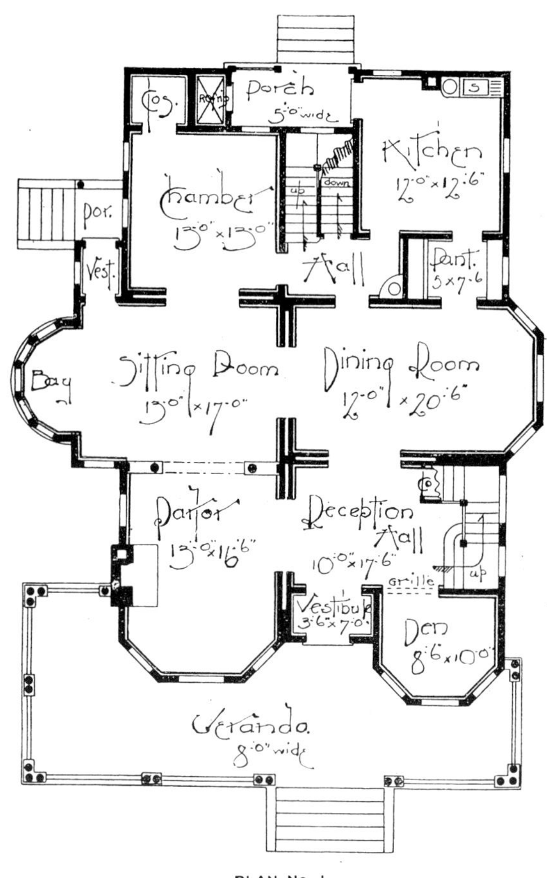

PLAN No. 1

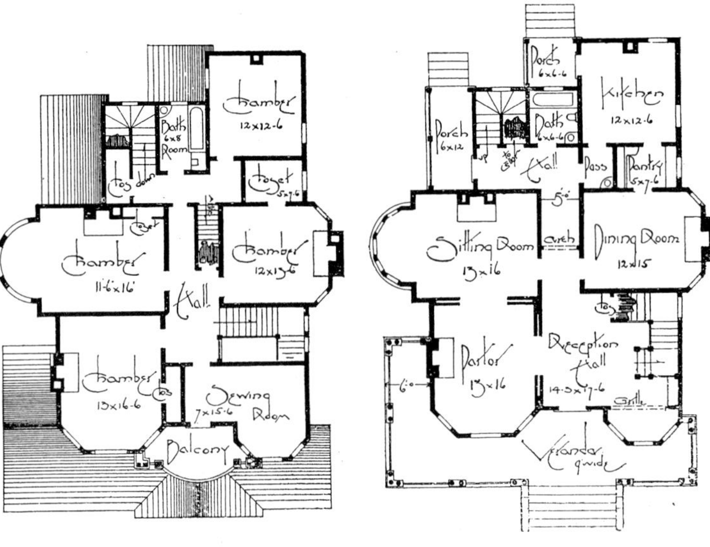

PLAN No. 2

In Plan No. 2 the arrangement is more as would be required in the South. The hall extending back from which we reach the kitchen, a convenient bath-room, back and cellar stairs and outside entrance. Further particulars will be given on application.

In Plan No. 1 the dining-room is made longer by taking up the width of the central hall shown in Plan No. 2. The cost is about the same for each plan.

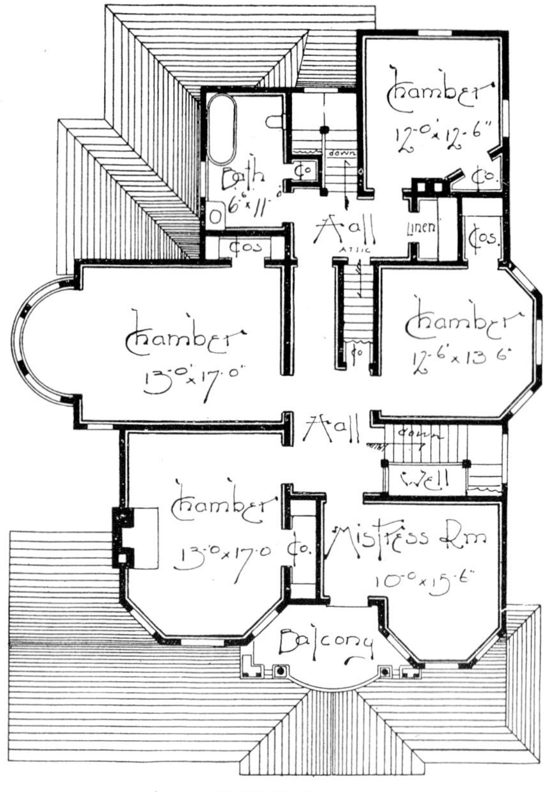

PLAN No. 1

FLOOR PLANS FOR DESIGN No. 31

A NEW, modified Colonial house, as handsome and convenient a design as can be made for the money. Every side abounds in beautiful features and good proportions. The plan can be modified to suit most any requirement.

The first story is weather-boarded; the second story, gables and roof are shingled. The hall and three rooms on first floor are in hardwood, the balance in Tennessee bright pine.

The tower-room can be used as a den or workshop for amateur photography, etc. A fire-place can be put in this room if required. The attic is large and light, but not finished complete at the price. Cellar under entire house. Width, 44 feet; length, 56 feet. Stories, 10 feet and 9 feet 2 inches.

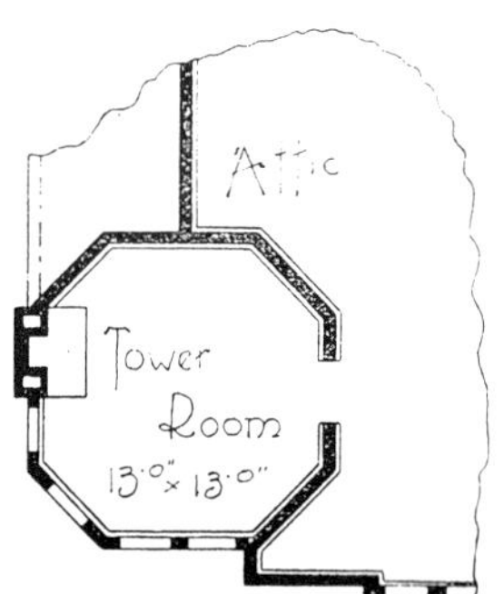

TOWER ROOM, THIRD STORY

DESIGN No. 31. **A BEAUTIFUL SUBURBAN PLACE—(COLONIAL RENAISSANCE)** *Geo. F. Barber & Co., Arcts*

COST, $5,800 TO $6,200

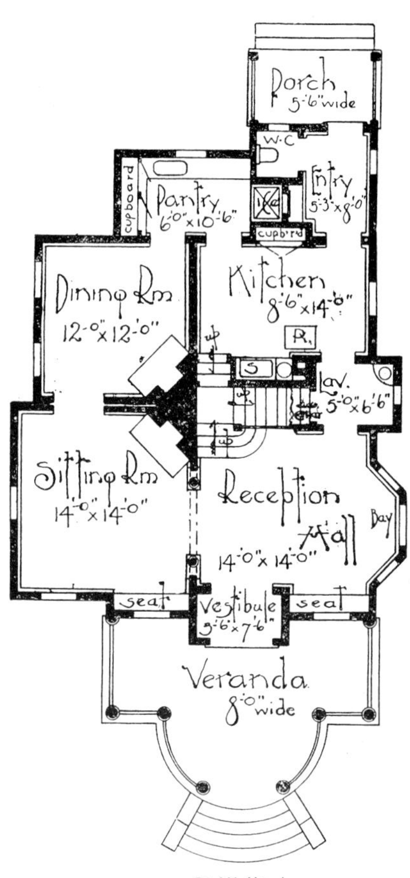

PLAN No. 1

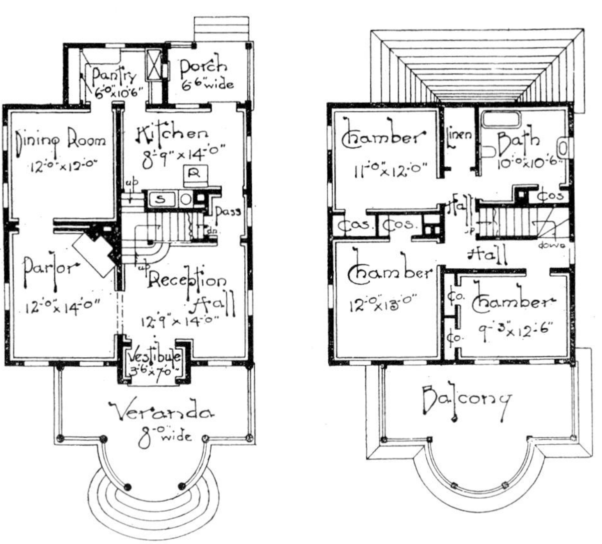

PLAN No. 2

Plan No. 2 is figured to be finished in natural pine or paint work, brick foundation, shingled roof and generally inexpensive treatment, yet durable and strong.

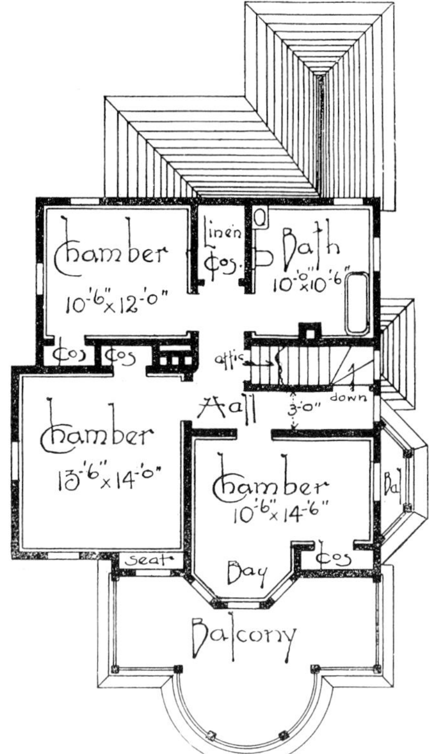

PLAN No I

FLOOR PLANS FOR DESIGN No. 32

THIS is one of our most delightful little Colonial homes, shown here in two sizes, the principal features being retained in each. A very nice reception hall, indeed, one that may be utilized as a sitting-room when desired. The stairs are neat and take up but little space, and are reached from the kitchen as well as from the hall. Under these stairs we pass through a convenient lavatory to the kitchen and to the cellar stairs.

The grouping of the kitchen sink, range and range boiler is of the best. A handy kitchen cupboard, the pantry with the ice chest set for icing from the outside, are all great conveniencies. The second story is complete in all requirements.

The front porch is in itself useful and attractive. The stories are 9 feet and 8 feet 6 inches. Cellar under kitchen, dining-room and back part. Oak finish is used for the hall and front room, the rest as desired by the owner.

DESIGN No. 32. A MODEST HOME—(COLONIAL) *Geo. F. Barber & Co., Arcts.*

COST, PLAN No. 1, $2,300 TO $2,600---PLAN No. 2 $1,900 TO $2,100

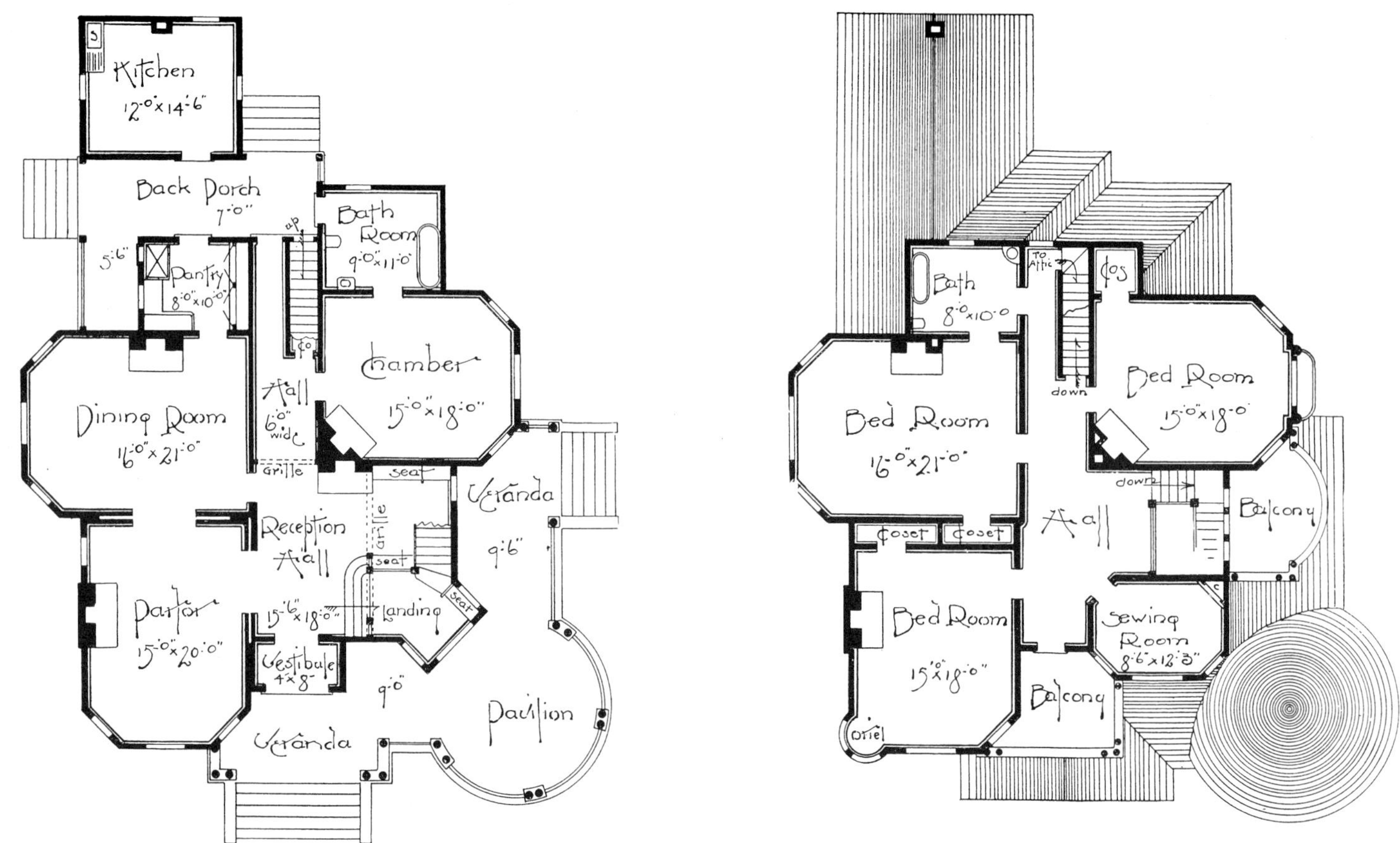

FLOOR PLANS FOR DESIGN No. 33

A Southern Home prepared for erection in a Southern city. The design contains many attractive features that can not be shown in the illustration. It has a corner reception hall with paneled ceiling. Rooms good size, with narrow hall through to rear. The veranda is a special feature, being very wide and cool in summer. The balconies also lend variety to the design in both beauty and comfort.

It is a frame house with 2x6 studding. Roof shingled. No cellar is included in the plan, yet as much cellar can be had as required at an additional cost of from $100 to $300. The open tower on third story can be reached from the attic and affords a good view over surrounding country. Size 55 feet front by 70 feet deep over porches in their widest extensions; stories, 11 feet and 9 feet 6 inches. The kitchen is detached but joined by a wide porch to main house.

DESIGN No. 33.

PLEASANT SOUTHERN HOME

Geo. F. Barber & Co., Arcts.

COST, $6,500 TO $7,000

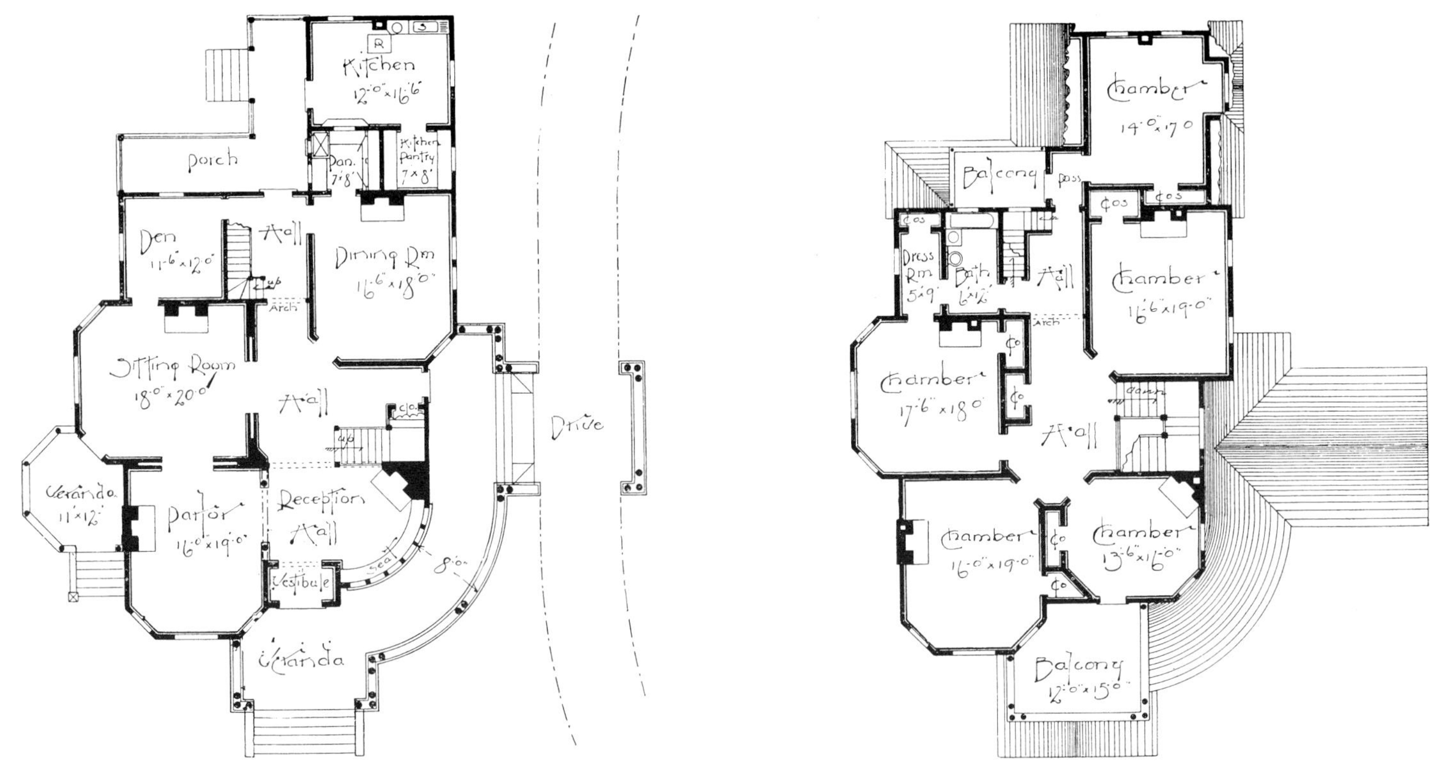

FLOOR PLANS FOR DESIGN No. 34

In the above illustration we have a home of many attractive features, both for the interior and exterior. The splendid veranda extends around from the front entrance to the side, where a convenient entrance is had to the hall opposite the porte-cochère. The large front hall in its unique arrangement must commend itself to all. The large front balcony and the open tower, third story, are features that give elegant effect and outlook.

The interior is treated for convenience and spacious rooms. The finish for the first floor is in hardwoods and natural pine for rooms above. A good cellar and furnace heat, besides grates, furnish ample warmth for winter months, and large rooms, high ceilings and good construction give a cool effect for the summer, making a most excellent Southern home. Height of stories, 11 feet and 10 feet 6 inches, respectively. Width of front, 57 feet.

DESIGN No. 34.

PHOTOGRAPHS SHOWING HOUSE AS BUILT AT GREENSBORO, N. C.

Geo. F. Barber & Co., Arcts.

COST, $5,800 TO $6,000

VIEW in the parlor, looking toward the front or octagon end of the room.

VIEW in the hall, showing the staircase and a grille; also showing circular window of the hall, under which is built a curved seat.

VIEW of the house from the northeast, as located on a beautiful hill overlooking the city, comprising some four acres.

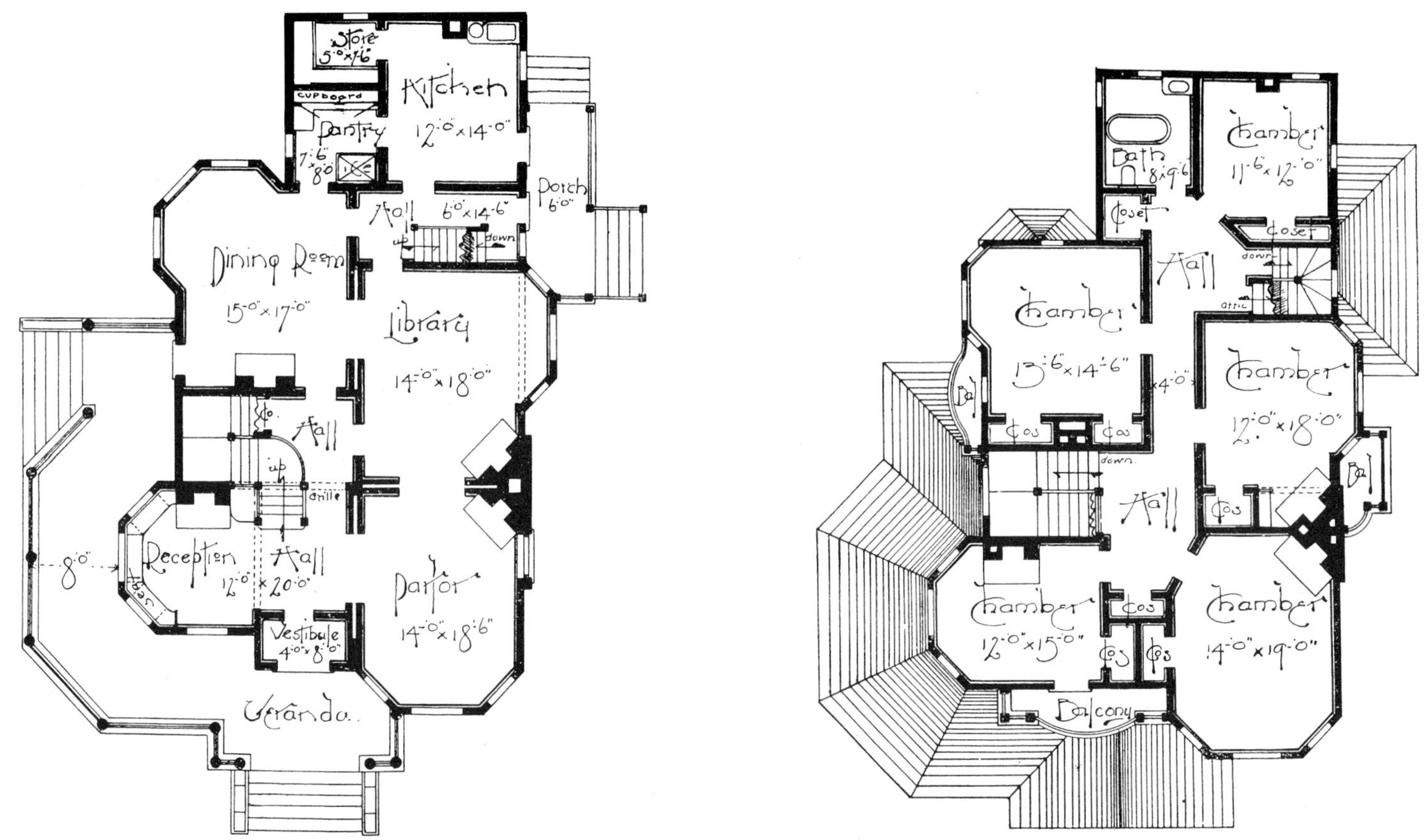

FLOOR PLANS FOR DESIGN No. 35

The Modern Reception Hall, large enough to be useful and broken enough to be made beautiful, is the pride of every housekeeper. Such is the hall of this design, and the entire plan has been studied for convenience and for good exterior effect. The proportions are good from every point of view. The large bay, 12 feet 6 inches across, gives a fine oblique view from the dining-room.

All rooms are large and well lighted, with handsomely designed windows. The cellar, 7 feet deep, extends under the entire house, with stone foundation. First story is weather-boarded, second story and roof shingled. Studding for external walls are 2 x 6 inches. The plumbing is of excellent character, as is also the hardware and glass. Dimensions on the ground are 51 feet front by 64 feet deep, over porches. Stories are 10 feet for the first and 9 feet 2 inches for the second.

The treatment of the hall may be changed as desired, but with the grille, which may be hung with curtains, a sort of partition is formed, cutting off the reception-room from the main hall, making the reception-room a most attractive retreat indeed. With this treatment below we get an excellent room above.

DESIGN No. 35.

A PROGRESSIVE HOME DESIGN

COST, $5,600 TO $6,000

Geo. F. Barber & Co., Arcts.

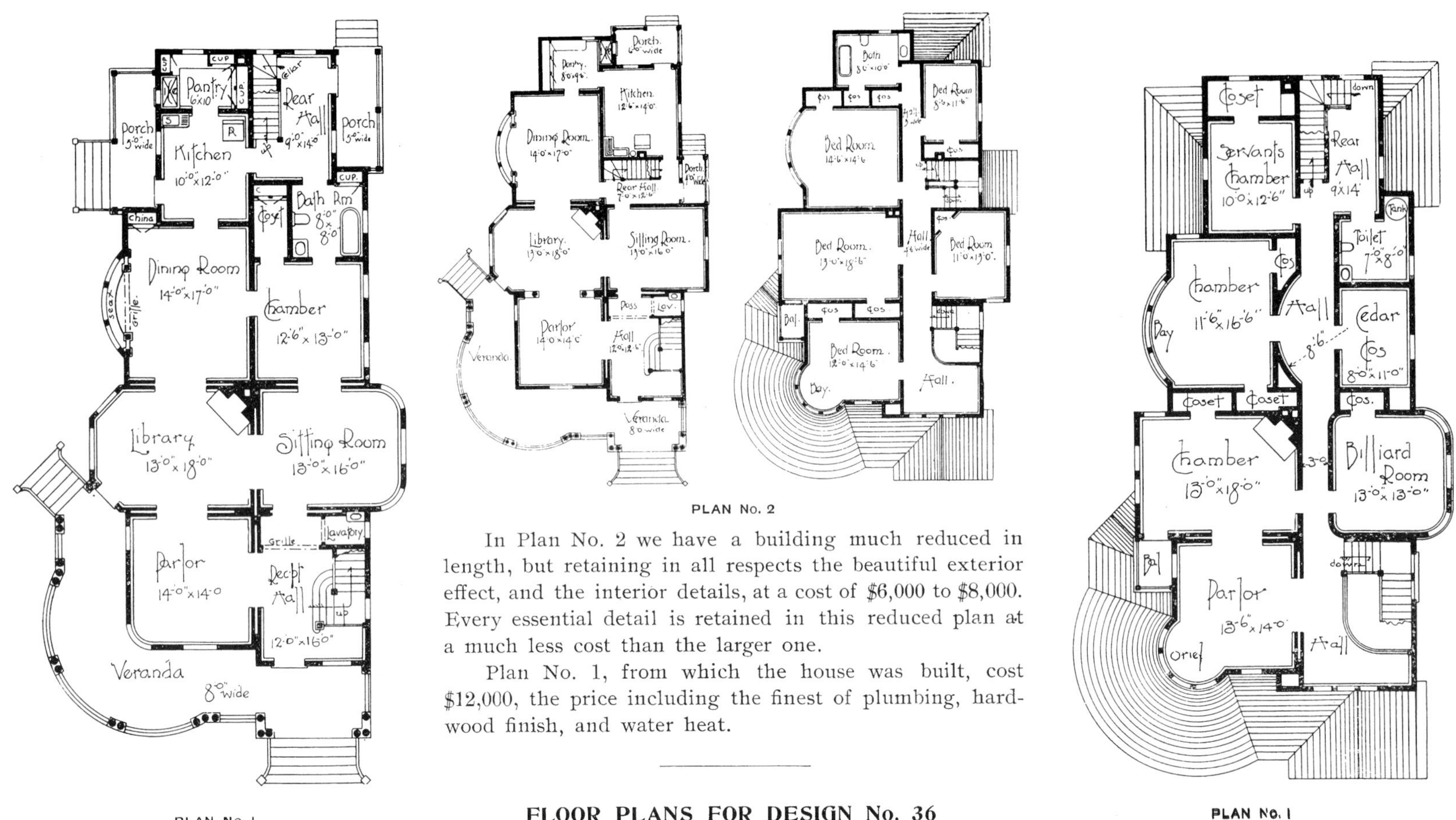

PLAN No. 2

In Plan No. 2 we have a building much reduced in length, but retaining in all respects the beautiful exterior effect, and the interior details, at a cost of $6,000 to $8,000. Every essential detail is retained in this reduced plan at a much less cost than the larger one.

Plan No. 1, from which the house was built, cost $12,000, the price including the finest of plumbing, hard-wood finish, and water heat.

PLAN No. 1

FLOOR PLANS FOR DESIGN No. 36

PLAN No. 1

Mr. C. E. Marr, the owner of this elegant home, visited our office for the purpose of personal consultation. The work of arranging the plans was, therefore, under his supervision, and he requested that the exterior appearance should be made as handsome as possible. The arrangement can, however, be changed to suit any requirements by those who wish to retain the outside effect, which is designed in beautiful harmony.

In Plan No. 2 we give another floor plan reduced in size suitable to the exterior treatment. Height of stories, 9 feet 6 inches and 9 feet, respectively, for both plans.

DESIGN No. 36. AMERICAN BEAUTY—RESIDENCE AT NEW HAMPTON, IOWA *Geo. F. Barber & Co., Arcts.*

COST $12,000

INTERIORS IN RESIDENCE OF C. E. MARR, PAGE 95

VIEW OF STAIRCASE LOOKING FROM PARLOR DOORS---
THE WOOD IS QUARTERED WHITE OAK

VIEW IN THE DINING-ROOM SHOWING GRILLE AND COLUMN
FINISH IN THE CURVED BAY

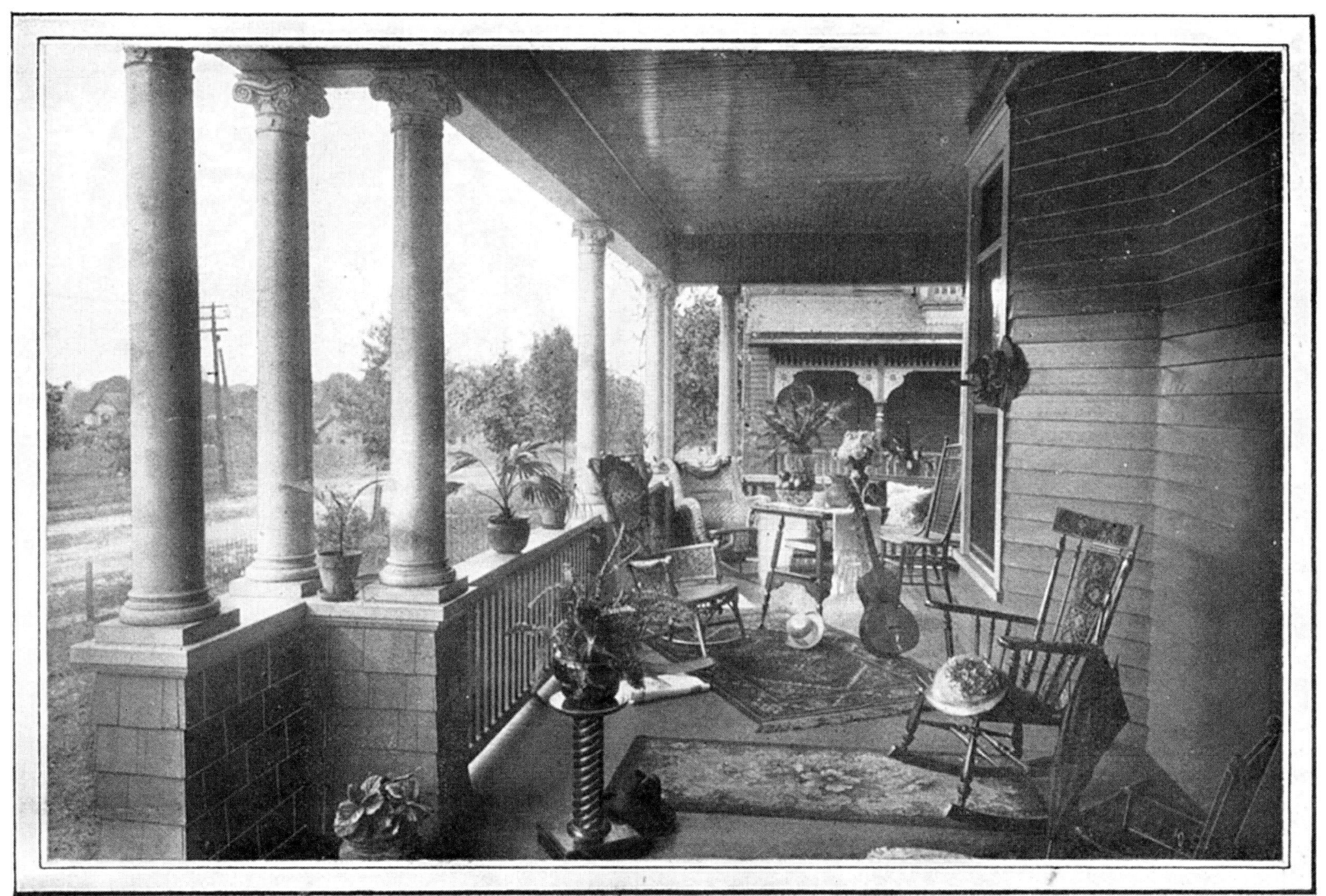

FURNISHED PORCH

FROM one of our Knoxville homes, showing the porch furnished for an afternoon tea and a generally chatty and musical reception. Nice architectural ideas are also furnished in columns, caps, balustrades, etc.

FLOOR PLANS FOR DESIGN No. 37

The style of this house is one much admired and will never wear out. The porch and balcony are prominent features and require tasteful treatment. The first story is weather-boarded, the second story, gables and roof, are shingled. Cellar under the entire house, with brick foundation. Hardwood interior finish, of neat design, is liberally used, and everything in the way of plumbing, glass, hardware, etc., is first-class. Size is 36 x 47 feet over porches. First is 10 feet, second story 9 feet 2 inches, cellar 7 feet. The cost of this house was more than that given above, but for the average our figures are close to correct.

One of the features of the plan is the sewing-room, so much desired by most house-keepers. It is convenient both from the sitting-room and back entrance, and indirectly to the kitchen. Five splendid sleeping rooms, with closets and bath, constitute a convenient second floor.

DESIGN No. 37. RESIDENCE AT ATTLEBORO, MASS. *Geo. F. Barber & Co., Arcts.*

COST $3,900 TO $4,400

LEFT PERSPECTIVE VIEW

THIS Ionic portico was recently erected in Knoxville for R. P. Gettys, Esq., adding it to an old Colonial structure built some fifty years ago. The house, not shown in cut, is large and roomy, the porch being in splendid proportion thereto. The columns in the main porch are some 22 feet high, and the smaller ones about half that. Both porches were built at once; being in reality but one single structure. The entire porch is painted white. Size of floor plan 22x61 feet. The structure, including foundation, cost about $1,700. To see the building as it stands in its imposing beauty one would think the house and all were built at the same time.

RIGHT PERSPECTIVE VIEW

A COLONIAL porch, having the unusual appearance of being built double.

COMFORT AND ARCHITECTURE

THE above porch was designed for the front of the residence of E. E. Mummert, Goshen, Ind., and shows what may be done in this line, either for new or old work. It cost about $500 as you see it.

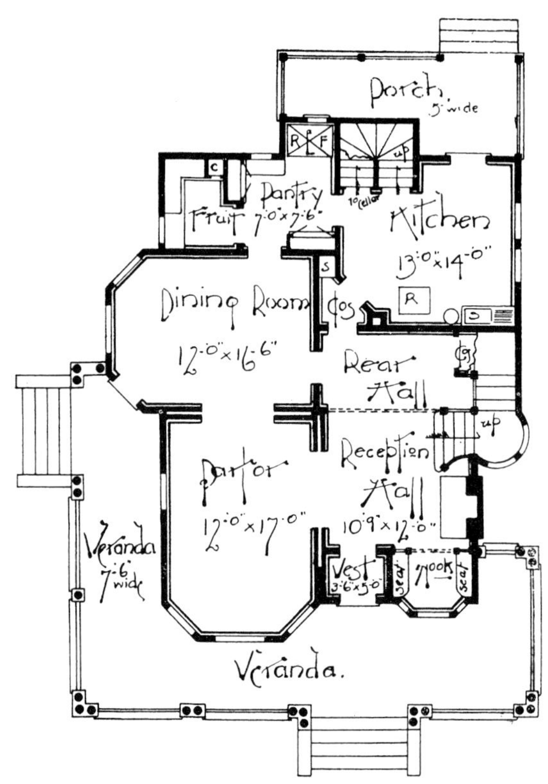

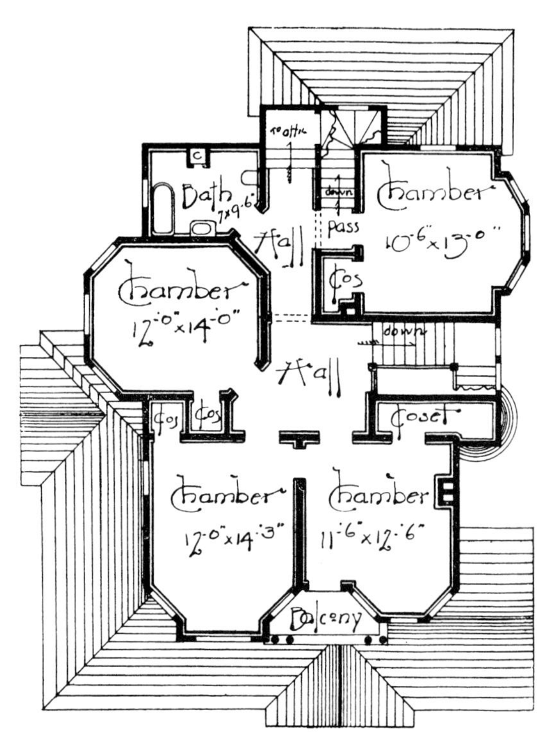

FLOOR PLANS FOR DESIGN No. 38

THE DESIGN is modern American and presents beautiful proportions from every direction. The cellar is under the entire house, with stone foundation. The hall is spacious and beautiful, and all other rooms arranged for convenience on both floors. A beautiful porch spans the entire front. The first floor rooms, exclusive of the kitchen and pantry, are finished in quartered oak, all the rest throughout is in white pine. Steam or hot water may be used for heating. Width 37 feet total. Stories 10 and 9 feet.

It is hard to imagine a more beautiful hall than the one arranged for this house, as one will see by a careful look at the plans. The pantry is double, one part to be used for fruit and a recess gives place for a refrigerator out of the way yet convenient to both kitchen and dining-room, and where it can be iced from the outside.

DESIGN No. 38. A SUBURBAN PRIZE DESIGN—(COLONIAL RENAISSANCE) *Geo. F. Barber & Co., Arcts*

COST, $3,800 TO $4,300

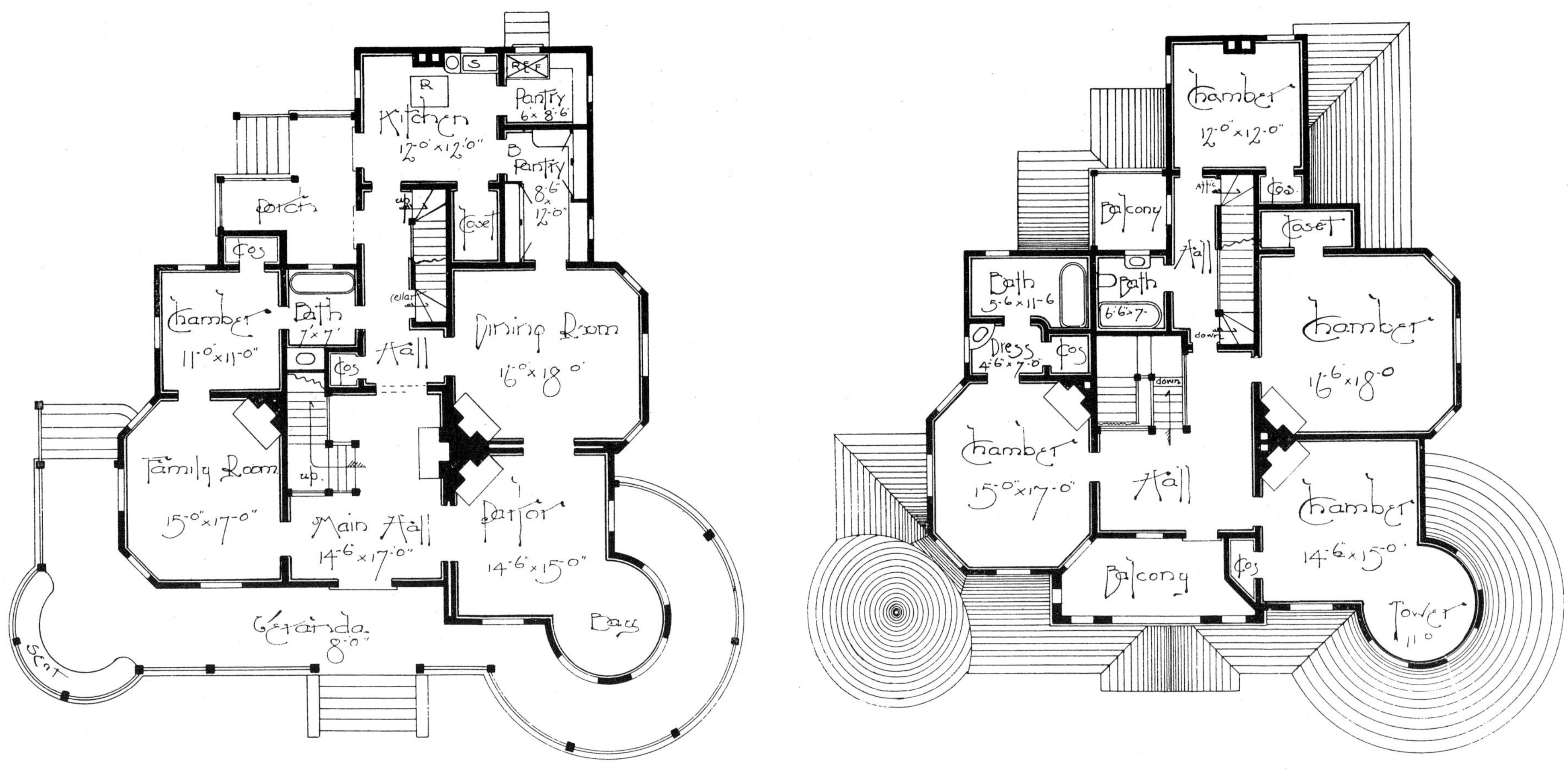

FLOOR PLANS FOR DESIGN No. 39

IN THIS design we have a wide central hall with large rooms on either side, thus making a broad front to the house. An eight-foot veranda extends entirely across and around the front, producing a handsome effect. A cosy balcony and a stately tower add life and dignity to the general design. It contains the elements of a good Southern home at the price, and may be enlarged if required. With artistically arranged grounds it will present the appearance of a veritable palace of elegance and refinement.

The bed-room and bath-room on the first floor will add to the convenience of the plan. A fire-place can be added to this room and the one above it, if desired, at a cost of perhaps $100.00. A cellar is under the back part of the house only, with brick foundation. Studding 2x6 inches is used in construction of outside walls, covered with sheathing and weather-boarding. Roof shingled. Beautiful hardware, glass and plumbing were used. Principal part of first story was finished in hardwoods, the rest in bright pine, natural finish.

The frontage of the house is 70 feet with a depth of 65 feet, with stories 11 and 10 feet, respectively.

DESIGN No 39. RESIDENCE OF DR. J. C. BROWN, DURHAM, N. C. *Geo. F. Barber & Co., Arcts.*

COST, $6,000 TO $6,300

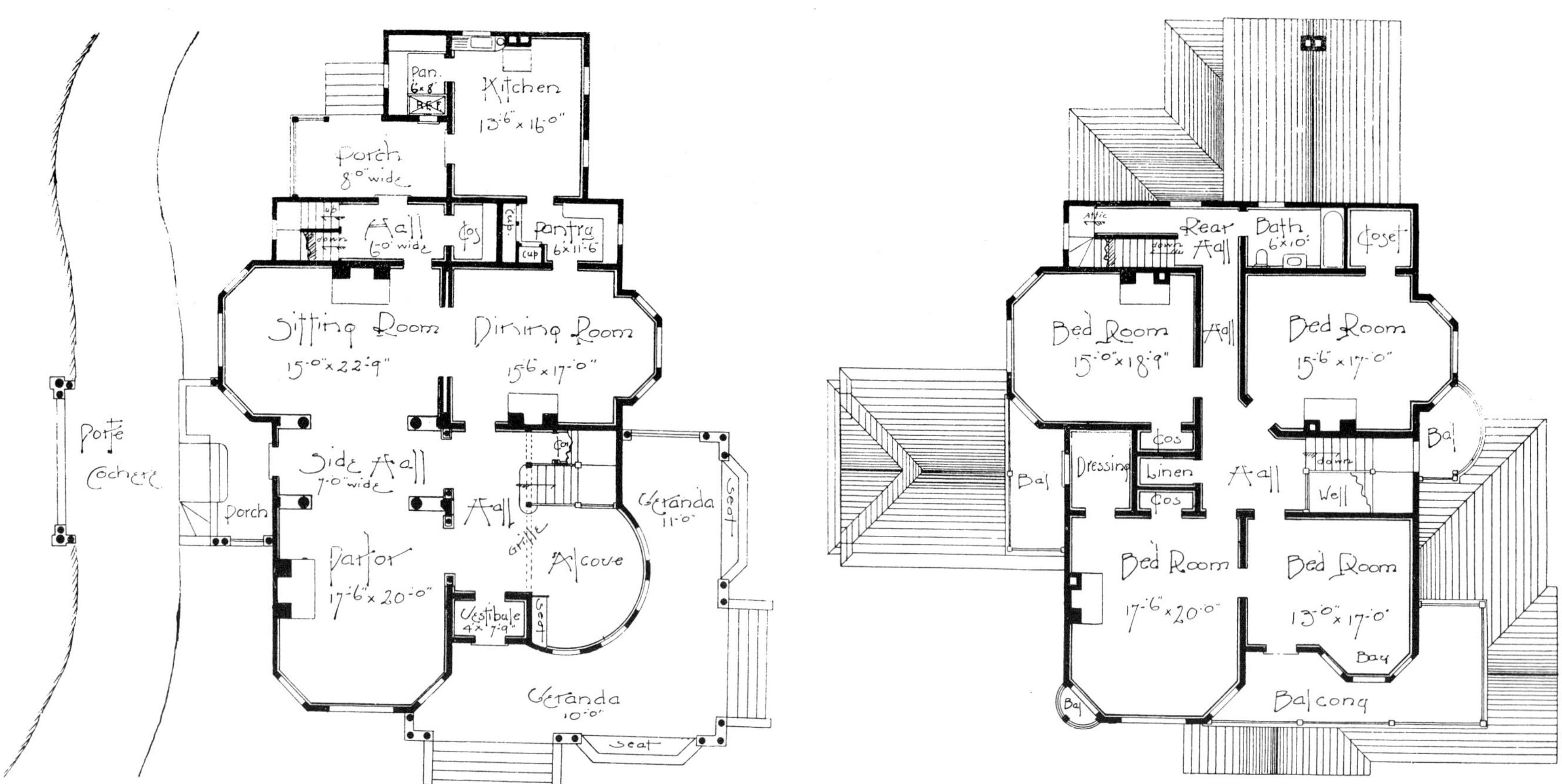

FLOOR PLANS FOR DESIGN No. 40

A CAREFUL study of this plan will reveal a number of nice features of convenience. The frame is 2x6 studding, sheathed, papered and weather-boarded. Roof slate. A good cellar is provided. Foundation is of brick. The exterior design will bear study, as the proprietor required a house of merit in every particular. Hardwood finish is liberally used for the inside, with natural bright pine for the second story. Dimensions, 45 feet 4 inches by 72 feet 4 inches, exclusive of porches. Stories are 11 feet and 10 feet, respectively.

The porch is quite novel as well as handsome. The hall is superb, with a reading alcove to the right of the entrance and a narrow hall leading to the porte-cochère on the left; it is so treated with columns and beams as to unite two of the principal rooms into one large and magnificent apartment. The whole treatment forms a desirable home and was erected for one of North Carolina's most worthy citizens, a son of Ex-Governor Thomas Holt.

DESIGN No. 40. **RESIDENCE OF CHAS. T. HOLT, HAW RIVER, N. C.** *Geo. F. Barber & Co., Arcts.*

COST, $6,200 TO $6,500

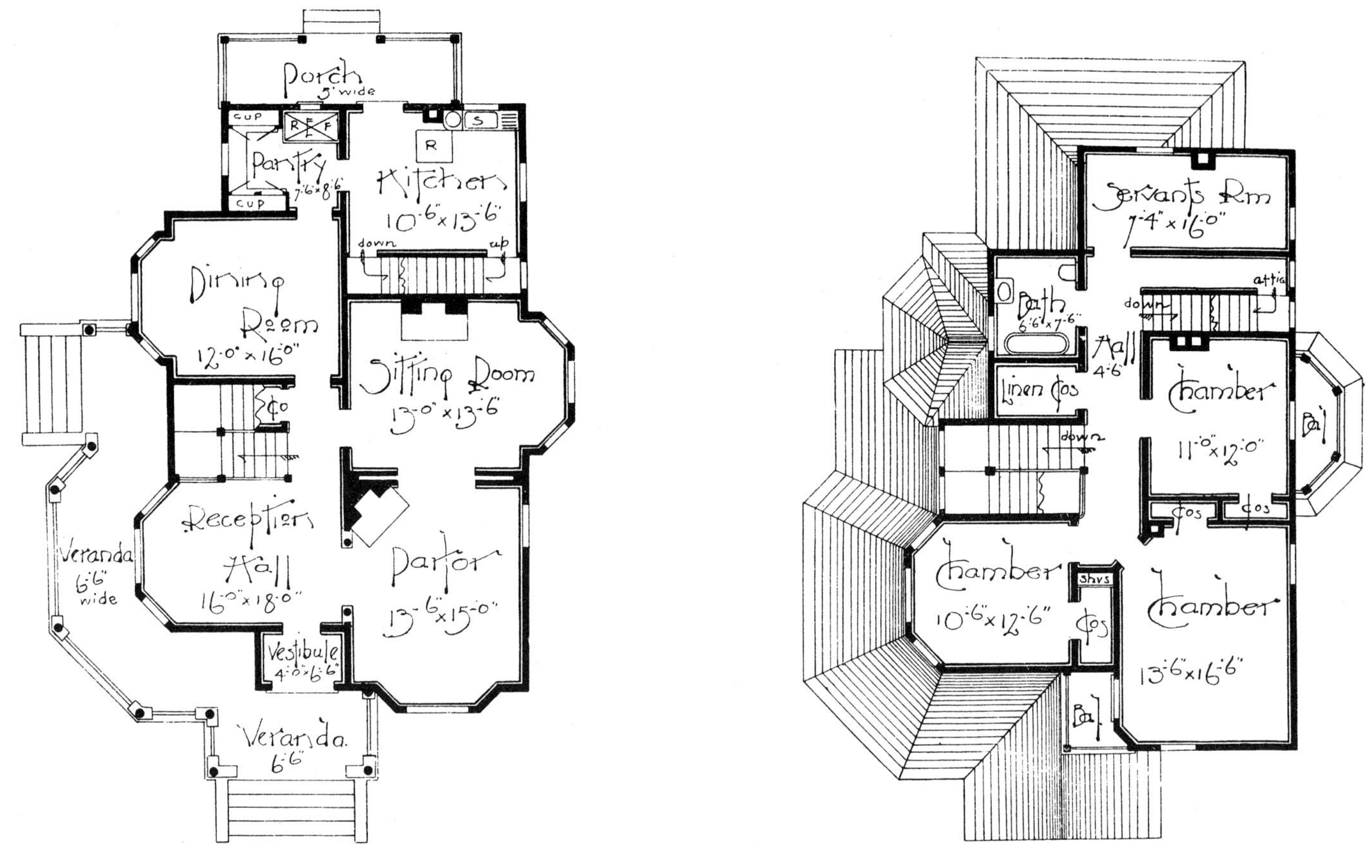

FLOOR PLANS FOR DESIGN No. 41

A HOUSE of beautiful proportions and pleasing effect. A spacious and handsome hall with many rooms constitute the plans, which are of excellent shape for convenience. In the large pantry is located the refrigerator, to be iced from the back porch, located convenient both to kitchen and dining-room and away from the heat of the kitchen. From the second floor, stairs lead to the attic in which one large room and a beautiful tower room may be finished.

The roof and second story are shingled, the rest is weather-boarded complete throughout. Width of structure over porches is 42 feet. Stories are 10 feet and 9 feet 2 inches in height. A good basement is provided for. Heater provisions, etc.

DESIGN No. 41.

RESIDENCE OF I. B. ZIEGLER, ESQ., KNOXVILLE, TENN.

Geo. F. Barber & Co., Arcts.

COST, $3,400 TO $3,800

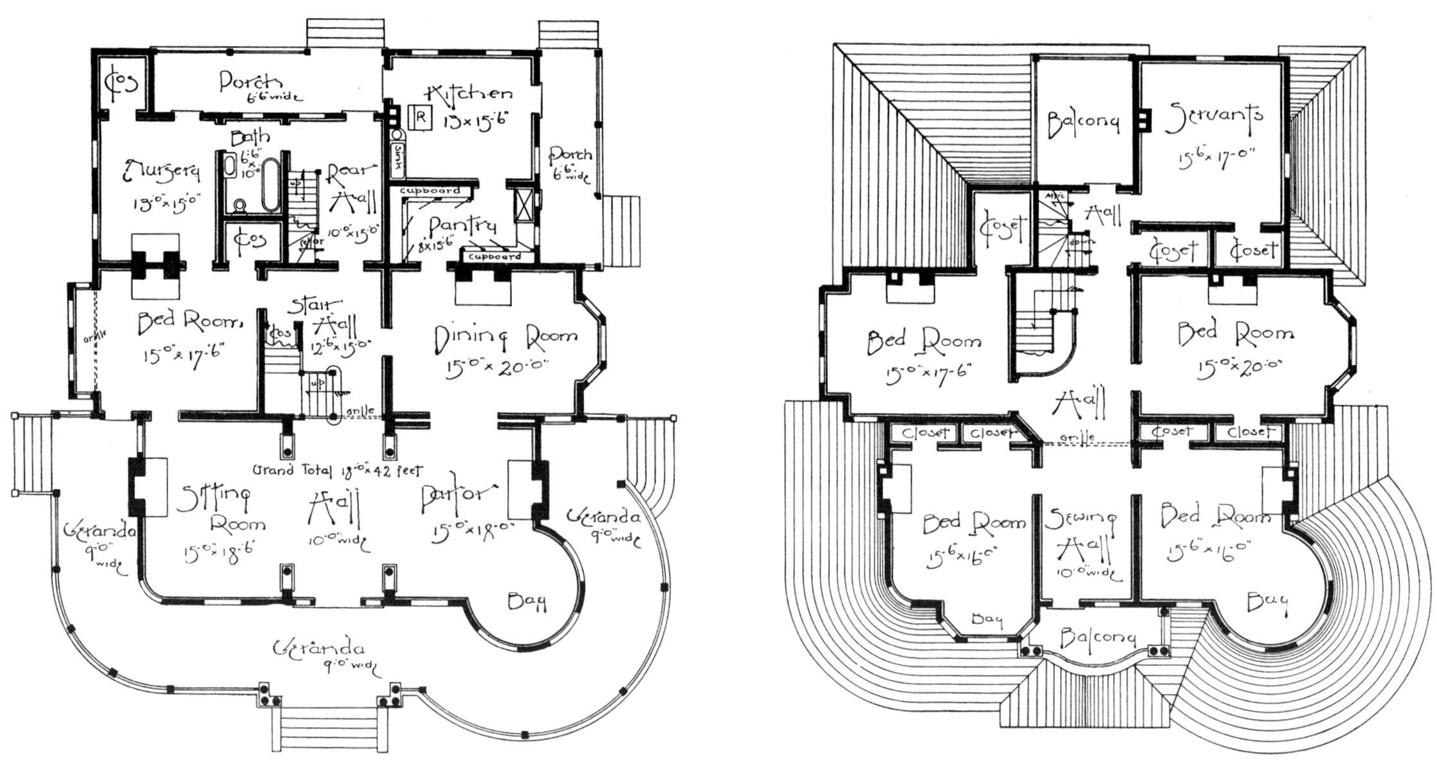

FLOOR PLANS FOR DESIGN No. 42

THIS HOUSE under some conditions can be built at a cost of a little less than $5,000, but in many localities would cost as much as $6,000. Provisions have been made on the first floor for complete living apartments, including baths, bed-room and nursery. A beautiful veranda surrounds the entire front, 9 feet wide.

The round corner on the sitting room extends to the roof, where it terminates in a picturesque turret, not shown in the cut being hidden by the large gable. Width of front over porches, 65 feet. Stories are 11 and 10 feet, respectively. Ash and quartered oak are the principal woods for interior on first floor, native pine in rear part and above.

The effect of the paneled beams spanning the space on either side of the front hall is to give to the front of the house one large room 42 feet long by 18 feet wide. The columns in the Ionic style rest on pedestals of dimensions suitable for the reception of decorative plants, etc. A specially designed grille cuts off the stair hall, but reveals a beautiful staircase uniting with the hall in a handsome way.

DESIGN No. 12.

MODERN SOUTHERN HOME

Geo. F. Barber & Co., Arcts

COST $6,500 TO $7,000

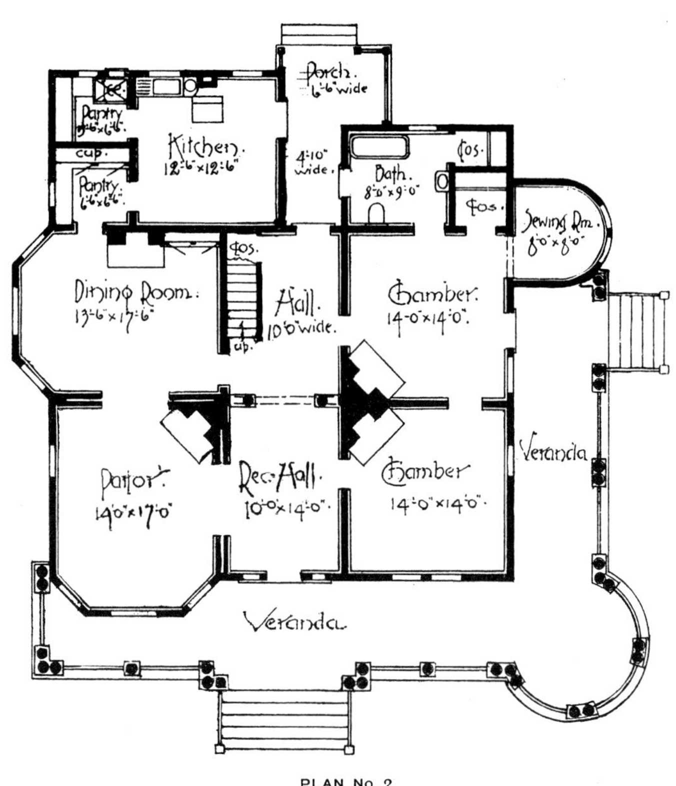

PLAN No. 2

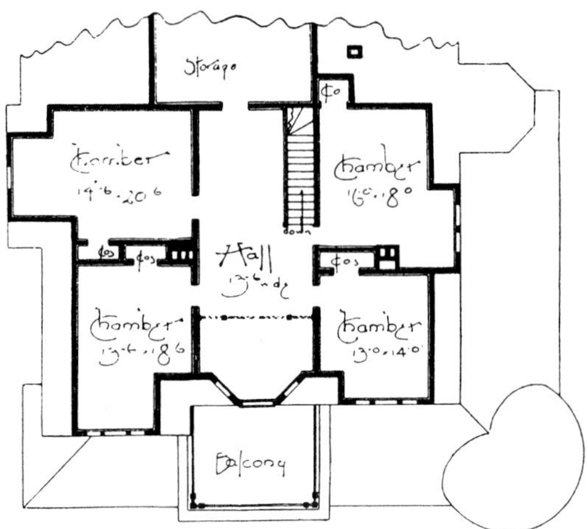

SECOND FLOOR, PLAN No I

FLOOR PLANS FOR DESIGN No. 43

THIS is one of our most beautiful, convenient and otherwise satisfactory houses of this class, portraying, as it does, a beautiful rendering of Colonial renaissance. A handsome roof and matchless porch constitute the main features of the exterior. An exceptionally wide centre hall is both comfortable and of excellent service as a sitting-room. The other rooms are spacious and well arranged for their several uses. Plan No. 2 is for a smaller and cheaper house.

Cost of Plan No. 1, $3,000 to $3,200. Cost of Plan No. 2, $2,500 to $2,800.

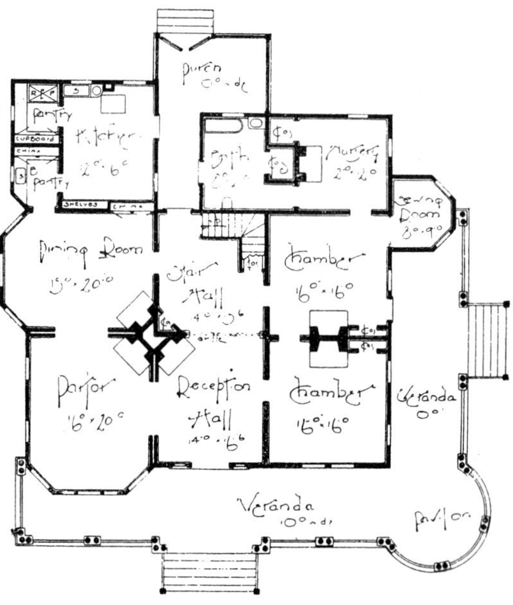

FIRST FLOOR, PLAN No. I

DESIGN No. 43.

A SUNNY SOUTHERN HOME

COST, $3,000 TO $3,200

Geo. F Barber & Co., Arcts.

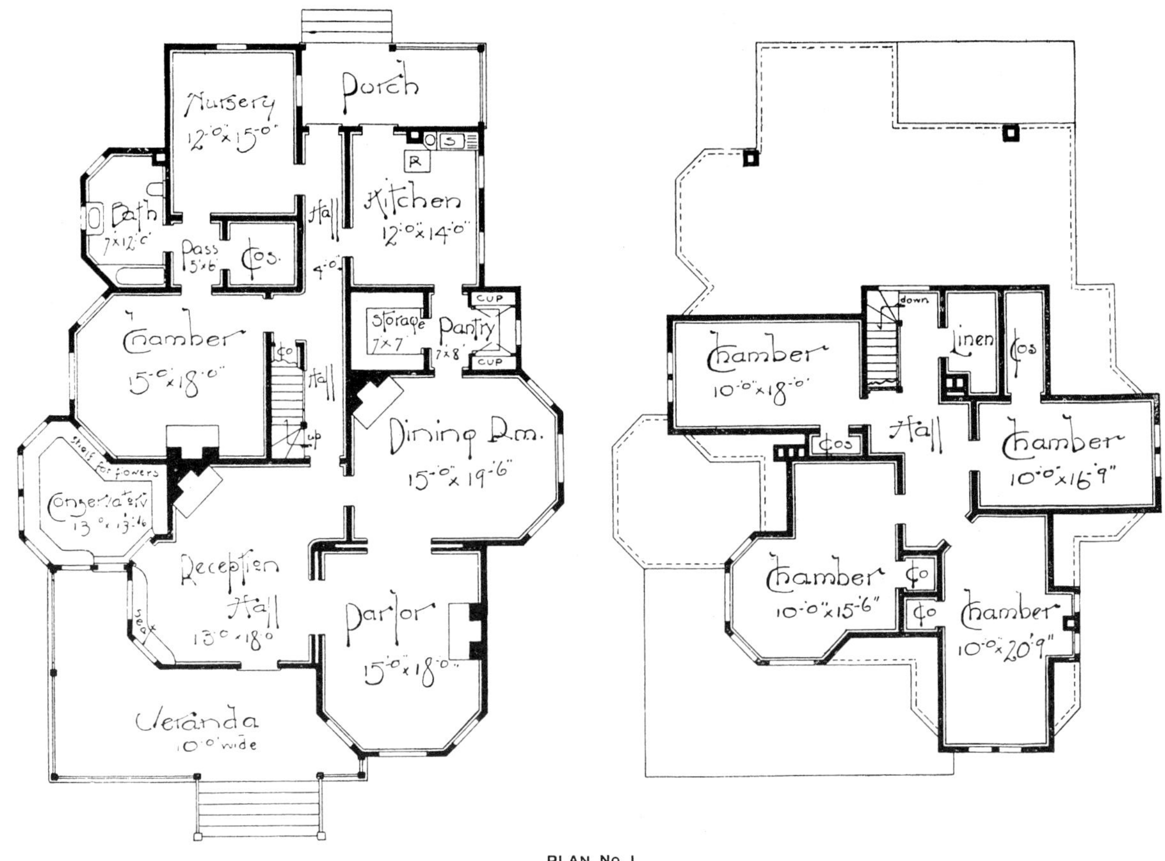

PLAN No. I

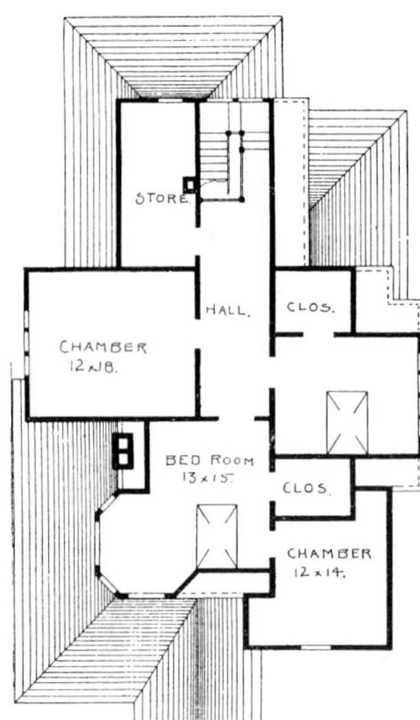

PLAN No. 2

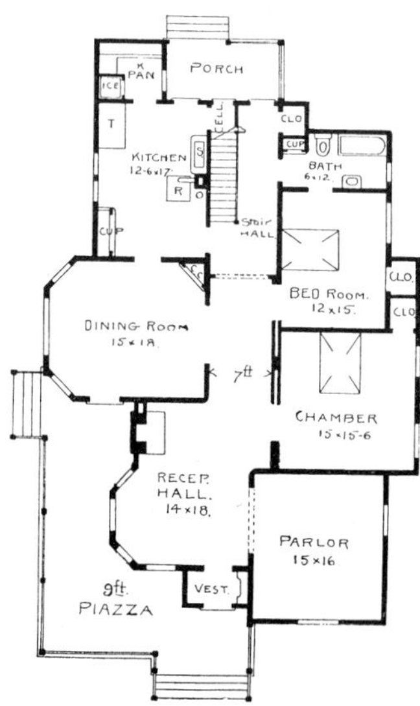

PLAN No 2

FLOOR PLANS FOR DESIGN No. 44

OF THE thousands who visit Tate Spring annually all admit that this is a most complete home. Rooms large and ceilings high admit of splendid embellishments. The reception hall is a perfect gem of a sitting-room, and a general convenience pervades the entire plan.

The house cost the proprietor $2,500, with attic not entirely finished, but first story finished entirely in oak, except kitchen. The arrangement is most satisfactory with all who have had any experience with it. It proves much more delightful as a home than one can see in the plans or even imagine. There is a small cellar. Brick foundation, shingle roof, and everything complete. Width 43 feet 6 inches, length 67 feet; stories 10 feet and 9 feet, respectively.

DESIGN No. 44. **RESIDENCE OF CLEM TOMLINSON, TATE SPRING, TENN.** *Geo. F. Barber & Co., Arcts.*

COST $3,000 TO $3,500

FLOOR PLANS FOR DESIGN No. 45.

The plans here shown are for a house 45 feet wide and 50 feet deep; over porches, stories 10 x 9-2 feet respectively, with complete and excellent finish throughout. Cost $4,500 to $4,800.

Price of Plans and Specifications, $65.00.

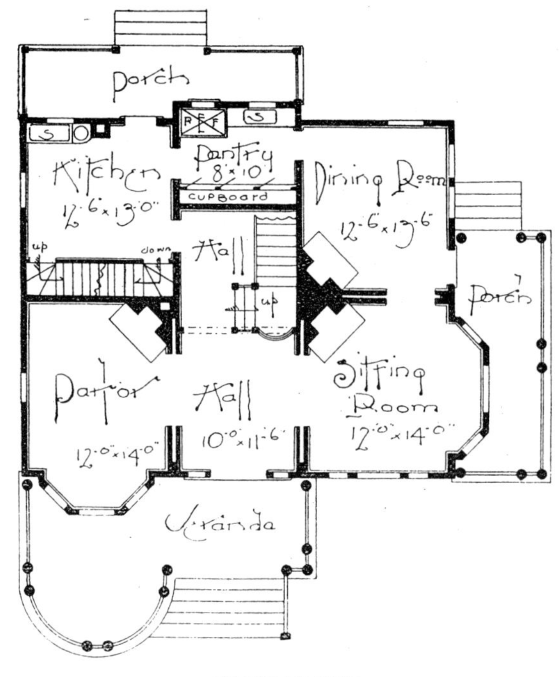

FIRST FLOOR

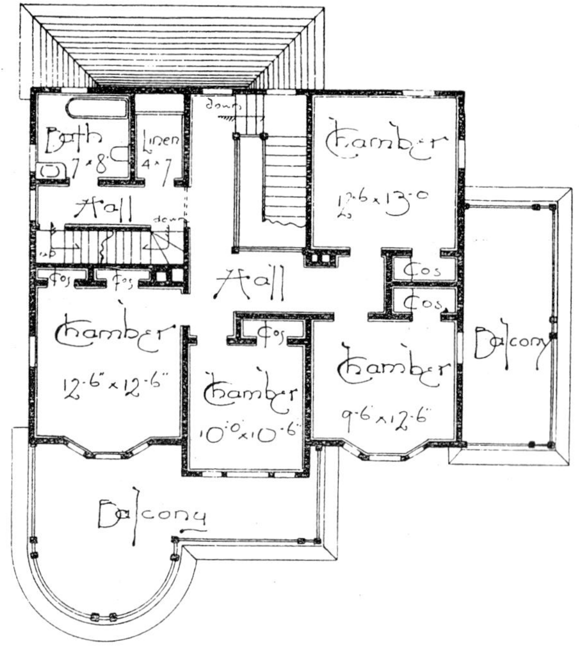

SECOND FLOOR

DESIGN No. 45. **COLONIAL ART** *Geo. F. Barber & Co., Arcts.*

Of all our Designs, this one is one of our most beautiful examples of Colonial Renaissance. The engraving is from a photograph and shows how beautifully and truthfully our working plans will develop into a finished structure.

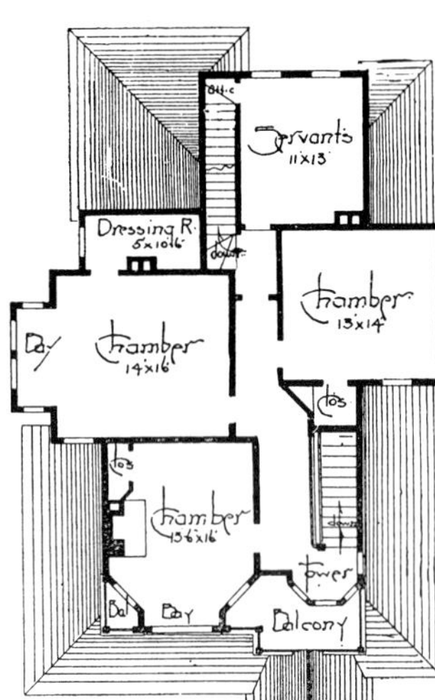

SECOND FLOOR PLAN

DESIGN No. 2-E.

RESIDENCE AT BELLEVILLE, KANSAS

Geo. F. Barber & Co., Arcts.

COST, $4,000 TO $4,500

BEAUTIFUL and extensive porches are a feature of the day, and when properly treated and well adapted to the general design there is nothing finer or more desired, as here shown.

The house has an admirable arrangement of five rooms on the first floor, with bath-room, closets, etc. The foundation is of brick, with cellar under all but hall and parlor. The roof is shingled. The walls are sheathed and weather-boarded with paper between. We have three entrances from the porch to the building, which is a great convenience.

The building is first-class all through. The stories are 10 feet and 9 feet 2 inches.

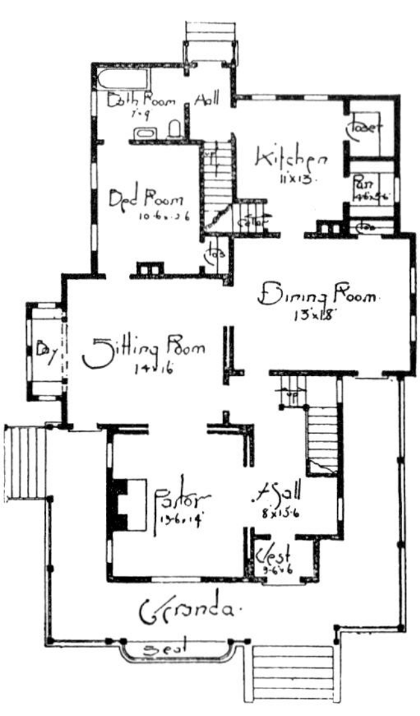

FIRST FLOOR PLAN

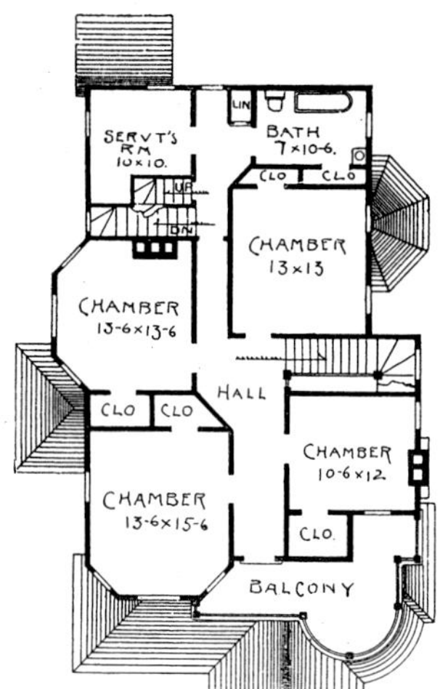

SECOND FLOOR PLAN

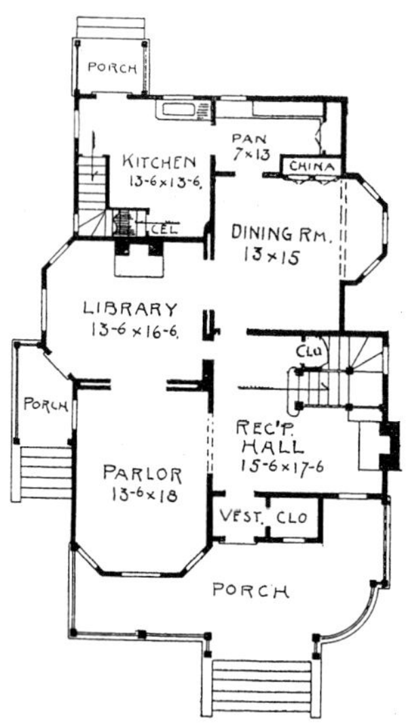

FIRST FLOOR PLAN

DESIGN No. 3-E. *Geo. F. Barber & Co., Arcts.*

RESIDENCE OF HON. CHURCH HOWE

COST, $5,000 TO $5,500

A FAVORITE among all lovers of beautiful homes. The residence of Hon. Church Howe, Auburn, Neb. Of good appearance from every point of view. Convenient and thoroughly studied floor plans. The principal features are the veranda, balcony, and general graceful outline of the roof, handsome windows, etc.

The plans may be varied to suit one's taste or purse. All the interior details are tasteful, and most of the rooms are finished in hardwoods, the rest in cheaper woods in local use. Hardware, plumbing and glass are specified with care for utility and finish. The house is frame, 2 x 6 studding, good cellar, stone foundation, shingled roof. Size—37 x 53 feet 6 inches. Stories, 10 feet and 9 feet 2 inches. Cellar, 7 feet.

This house was built at Hopkinsville, Ky., in 1898, for $3,400.

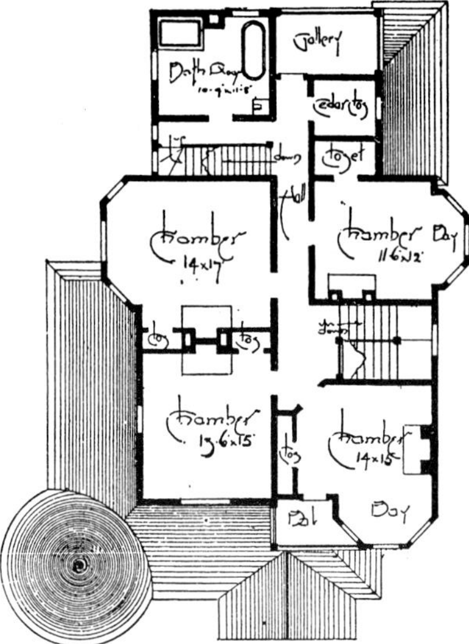

SECOND FLOOR PLAN

DESIGN No. 4-E. *Geo. F. Barber & Co., Arcts.*

RESIDENCE OF D. Y. GREIB, MISSIONARY RIDGE, TENN.

COST. $4,000 TO $4,500

THE PLAN and design were both prepared for a beautiful corner lot upon which the house was built. The hall is decorated with handsome grille work, a view of which is shown in the circle on page 72. The four principal apartments of the first floor are finished in hardwoods. The rest of house throughout is in the native, bright pine, of which there is nothing superior of an inexpensive nature.

Everything in connection with this beautiful home is first-class. A nice cellar is provided under the main part of the house. The cost includes a slate roof, good glass and first-class plumbing. The size of house is 47 feet by 63 feet over the widest extensions of the porch. Stories are 10 feet 6 inches and 10 feet.

So satisfactory was this house that Mr. Greib has, by his influence, been the means of a number of his friends placing their work in our hands.

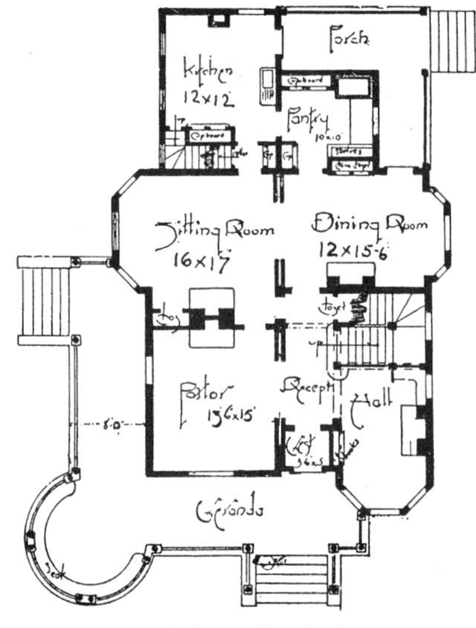

FIRST FLOOR PLAN

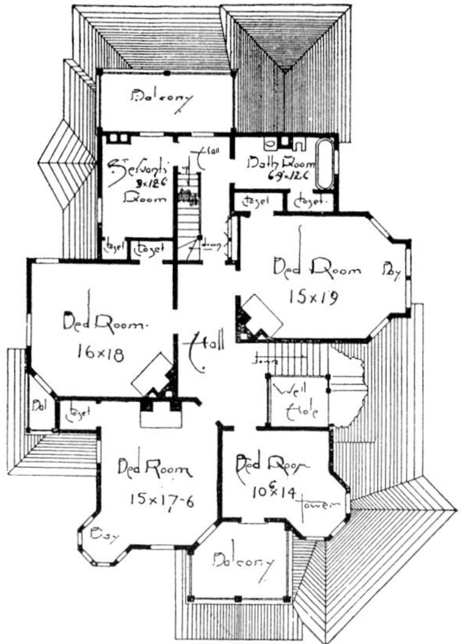

SECOND FLOOR PLAN

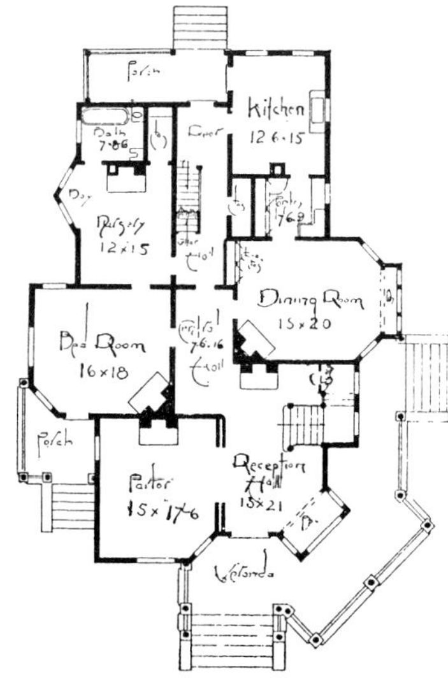

FIRST FLOOR PLAN

DESIGN No. 5-E.

A SOUTHERN HOME

Geo. F. Barber & Co., Arcts.

COST, $6,000 TO $6,500

THIS DESIGN was prepared for erection at Wilson, N. C., and has many features required in a Southern home, but may be arranged to suit any climate. The style is modern and artistic, all sides containing special features of design, forming beautiful contrast as viewed from various standpoints.

The kitchen is detached, but has covered porch between it and main house. There is a small cellar. Brick foundation. 2x6-inch studded walls, sheathed, papered. First story weather-boarded. Roof and gables and second story shingled with cypress shingles. Parlor, hall and dining-room finished in hardwood, balance in bright pine, natural finish. Size—52 feet front by 72 feet deep over widest extent of porches. Stories 11 and 10 feet, respectively.

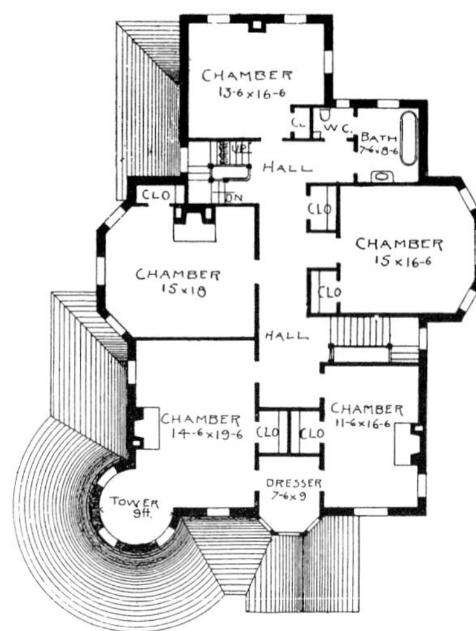

SECOND FLOOR PLAN

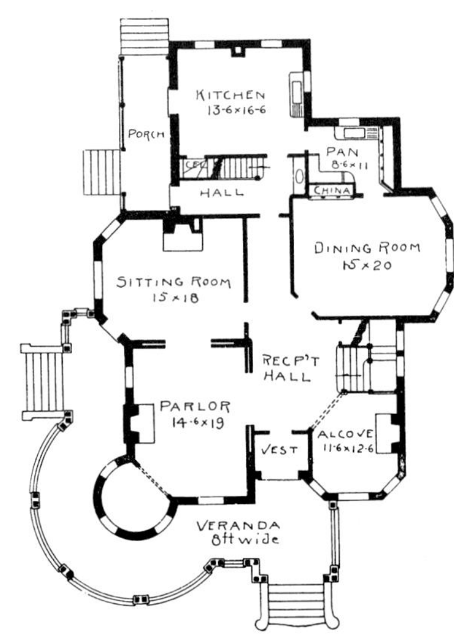

FIRST FLOOR PLAN

DESIGN No. 6-E. *Geo. F Barber & Co., Arcts.*

RESIDENCE OF HON. JNO. GILLIES, BRÆSIDE, CAN.

COST, $7,000 TO $7,500

THE FRAME of this house was of 2 x 6 studding, sheathed and papered and veneered with brick, floors doubled, and every precaution taken to keep out the cold winds. The roof is shingled. Foundation stone, hollow walls. Cellar under entire house. Steam heat. Main part of first story finished in hardwoods. All interior material and finish is good.

The stately tower, encircled by a broad, handsome veranda, is a special feature, giving the whole house a commanding appearance. For durability and good effect, stone is largely used in the construction of the veranda. Size—56 feet front by 72 feet deep. Stories are 10 feet 6 inches and 10 feet, respectively.

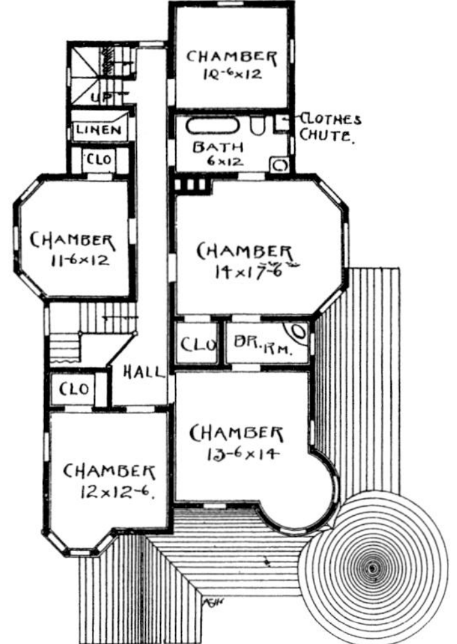

SECOND FLOOR PLAN

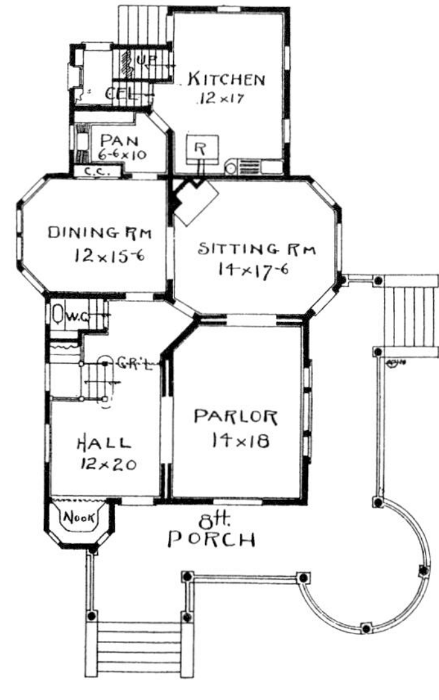

FIRST FLOOR PLAN

OLD STYLE NEW STYLE

DESIGN No. 7-E. *Geo. F. Barber & Co., Arcts.*

AN IOWA HOME

COST, $5,000 TO $5,500

A HANDSOME house, standing out in marked contrast with the older style. An elegant porch for furnishing for evening or afternoon receptions. The floor plan is complete in every detail. A good cellar, sufficient for all needs, is under the back stairs, at a landing of which a door admits one from the outside. Stone foundation, shingled roof, and everything complete. Width 39 feet over porch. Stories 10 feet and 9 feet 2 inches, respectively.

DESIGN No. 8-E. *Geo. F. Barber & Co., Arcts.*

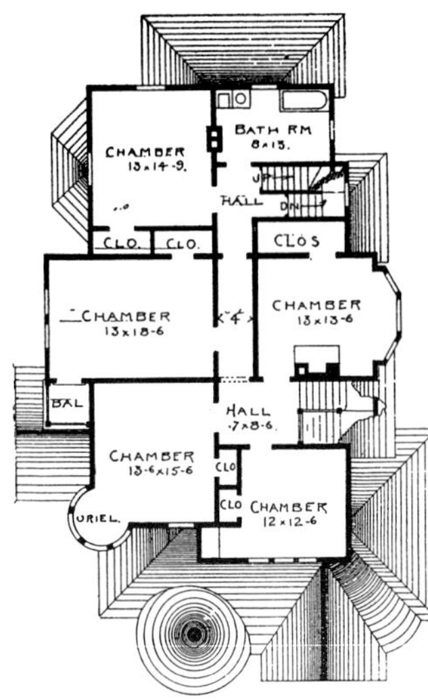

SECOND FLOOR PLAN

RESIDENCE AT BLANDINVILLE, ILLS.

COST, $6,500 TO $7,000

THIS HOUSE proves satisfactory, both in plan and appearance, wherever erected. Ten rooms are conveniently arranged, five on each floor. The front hall and veranda are special features, both for design and comfort.

The throwing together of the four principal rooms and hall produce most beautiful effects. Hardwood finish is used for these rooms, trimmed with neat, modern hardware, in keeping with the woods. Cellar under part of the house, back of parlor and hall.

Stone foundation. Shingled roof. Size—47 feet frontage by 71 feet deep. Stories are 10 feet for first floor and 10 feet for second floor. Cellar, 7 feet.

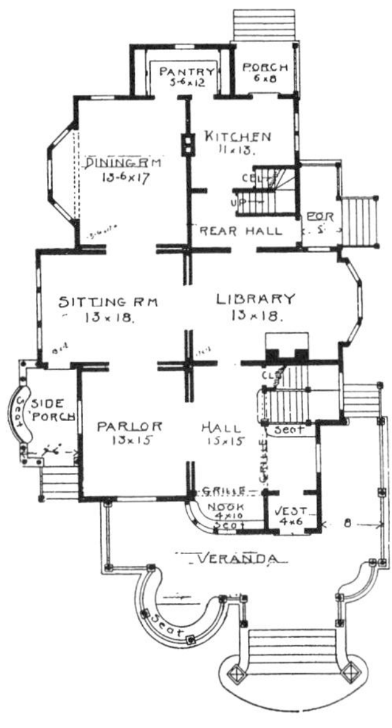

FIRST FLOOR PLAN

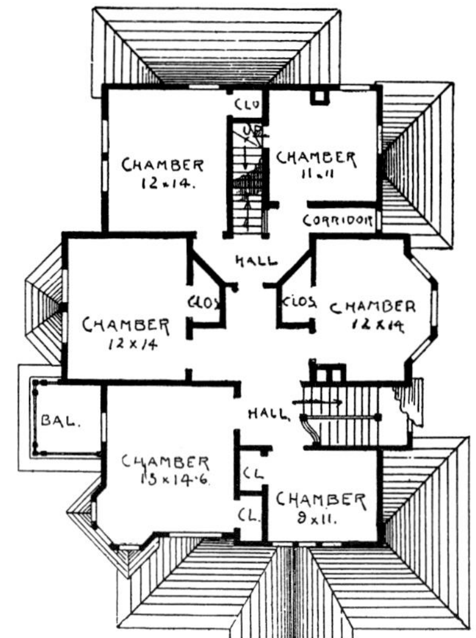

SECOND FLOOR PLAN

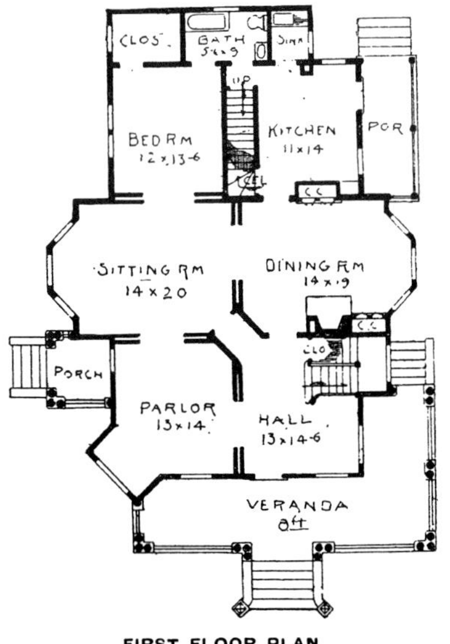

FIRST FLOOR PLAN

DESIGN No. 9-E.

RESIDENCE AT KENYON, MINN.

Geo. F. Barber & Co., Arcts.

COST, $4,000 TO $4,500

IN THIS beautiful Minnesota home the owner has many handsome features and much comfort, concerning which he writes us a splendid letter. There is a cellar under the entire house, with stone foundation. Furnace heat. With five rooms on the first floor, we can have one of them for a bed-room, and this requires a closet and bath-room, which we have provided in ample size—the bath being 5 feet 6 inches by 9 feet, and the closet 5 feet 6 inches by 7 feet 6 inches. The many porches give nice effect to both sides of the house, and a beautiful roof crowns the entire structure. The interior finish is mostly of hardwood, and with the three sets of sliding doors the entire first floor can be thrown into one grand apartment. Height of first story is 10 feet; second story, 9 feet 2 inches. Width of front, 43 feet over porches.

DESIGN No. 10-E. *Geo. F. Barber & Co., Arcts.*

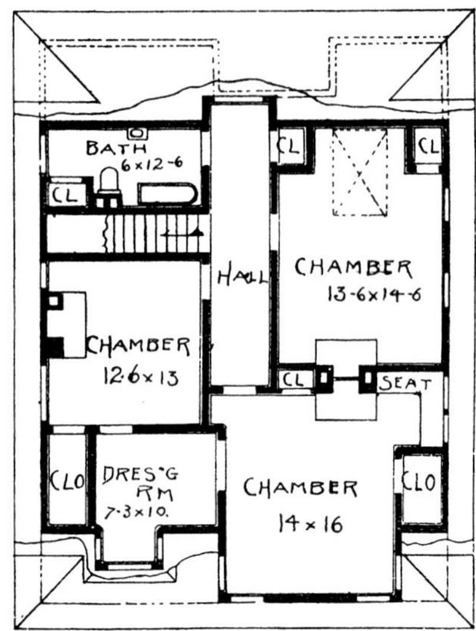

SECOND FLOOR PLAN

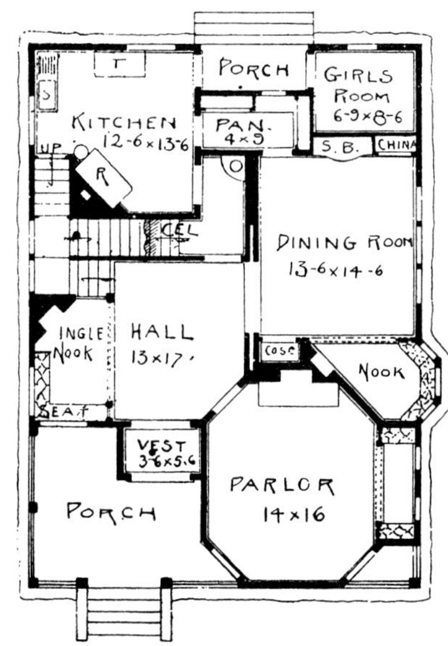

FIRST FLOOR PLAN

A COTTAGE OF SWISS PERSUASION

COST, $3,000 TO $3,500

AN ARTISTIC and well arranged house, suitable for an isolated place, say a location in the woods or in a rocky place—an outing cottage, as it were.

The hall is elegant, and each room has some attractive feature to add to its convenience and beauty.

Size—32 feet by 43 feet. Stories 9 feet and 8 feet 6 inches. Good cellar. All well built.

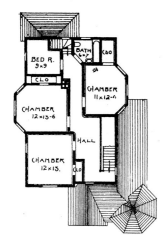

SECOND FLOOR PLAN

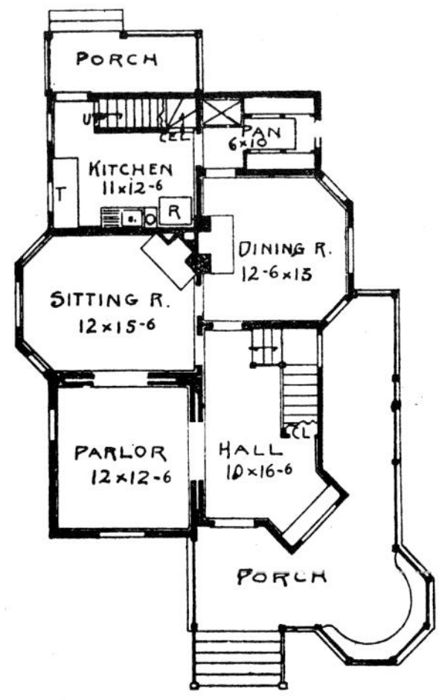

FIRST FLOOR PLAN

DESIGN No. 11-E. **RESIDENCE OF A. Y. BURROWS** *Geo. F. Barber & Co., Arcts.*

COST, $3,000 TO $3,300

RESIDENCE of A. Y. Burrows, Esq., Knoxville, Tenn., a house both attractive and convenient. The hall and three principal rooms are finished in oak, the rest in native, bright pine; was built upon a 50-foot inside lot, but is best adapted to a corner.

The first story is weather-boarded, the second story and roof are shingled. Foundation stone, with small cellar. The staircase was arranged so as to give large space at front of hall, where it affords a splendid view through a large, handsome window. The parlor window is plate and art glass, 54 inches wide.

Specifications call for a complete house, and makes a highly satisfactory home in every particular. Size—39x61 feet over porches, with 10 foot and 9 feet 2 inch stories, respectively.

DESIGN No. 12-E. **MODERN HOME IN STONE AND FRAME** *Geo. F. Barber & Co., Arcts.*

COST, $11,000 TO $12,000

THE above design calls for cobble-stone for the first story, with frame for the second—the frame part being covered with slate, as is also the roof. The basement is carried under the entire house 7 feet and all well finished up, one part containing a cold storage room for fruits and vegetables, a laundry with three tubs, servants' bath-room, a room for fuel and hot water heater.

An elegant veranda spans the front and left sides, and a large carriage porch adorns the rear of the structure. In the dining-room opposite the grate the buffet and all the doors and windows, on either side, are built in one solid piece of oak finish, the ceiling of room is paneled in oak, and the same beautiful finish is carried throughout.

The tower is carried up in stone to the frieze line, under a conical roof of splendid proportions. The same design could be carried out in most any scale or of any materials. The width of the front is 54 feet over the extremities of porches and bays. Stories, 10 feet 9 inches, and 9 feet 6 inches, respectively.

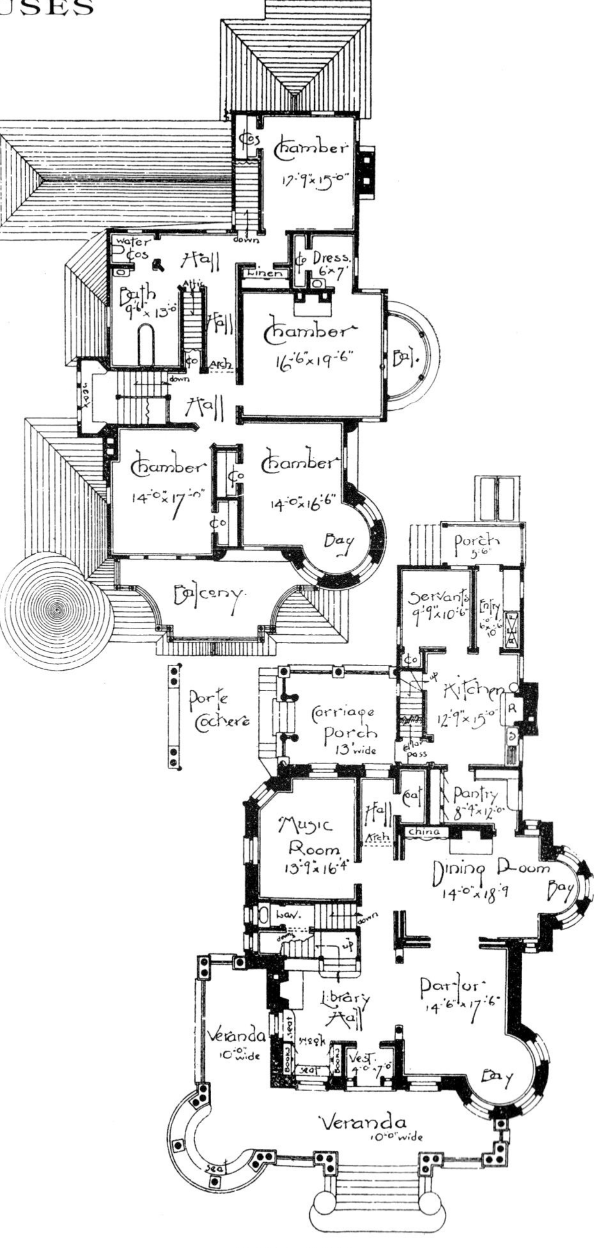

FLOOR PLANS

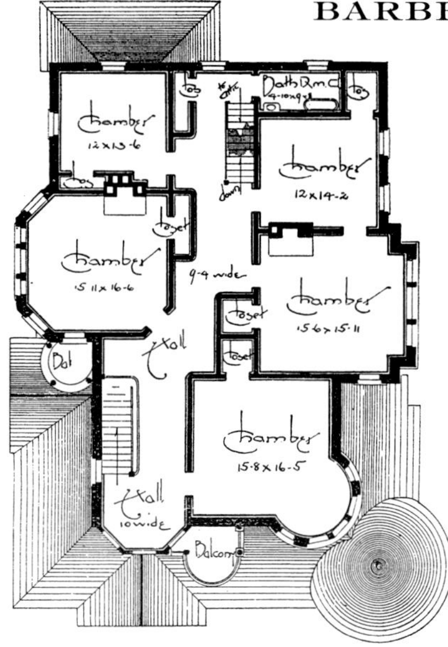

SECOND FLOOR PLAN

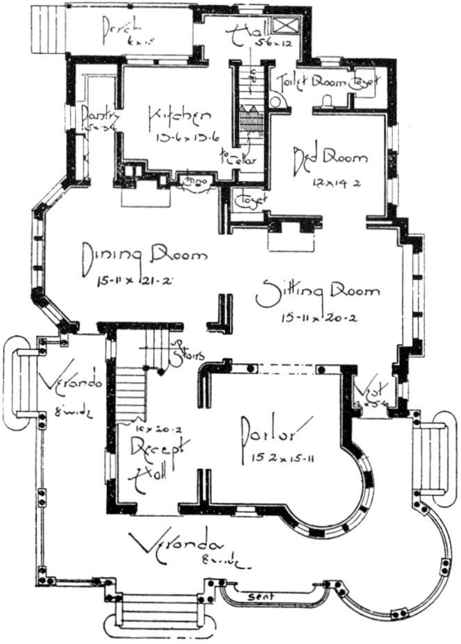

FIRST FLOOR PLAN

DESIGN No. 13-E. **MODERN RESIDENCE IN BRICK** *Geo. F. Barber & Co, Arcts.*

COST, $8,000 TO $9,000

THIS beautiful home has features of attraction from every point of view; is modern, up-to-date in style, and will always remain pleasing to the observer. The porch is massive, beautifully broken in plan, and wide enough to be of excellent service.

The house is brick veneered, slate roof, with proper trimmings; buff brick with stone trimmings were used. Stone foundation, with cellar under entire house. Steam heat. The hall, dining-room and bed-room are finished in quartered white oak, the parlor in white or silver birch, library in quartered sycamore; all the rest of the rooms in natural pine. Gas and electricity throughout. Glass, hardware and plumbing of the best. Beautiful windows are designed in every room.

By building this house in frame, with less elaborate interior, the price could be gotten down some $5,000 from the above. Size—49 feet front by 56 feet 6 inches deep. Stories 10 feet and 9 feet, respectively.

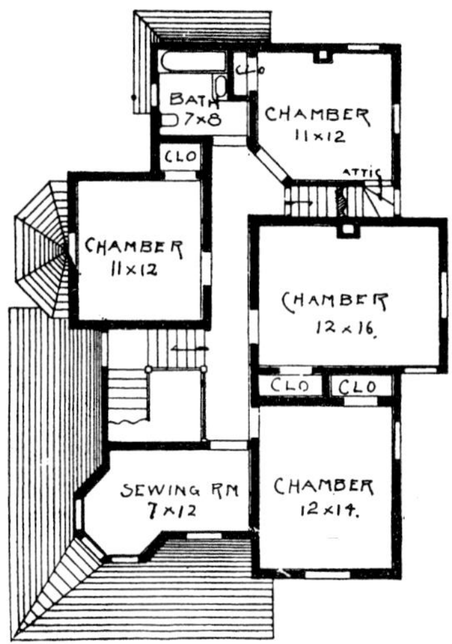

SECOND FLOOR PLAN

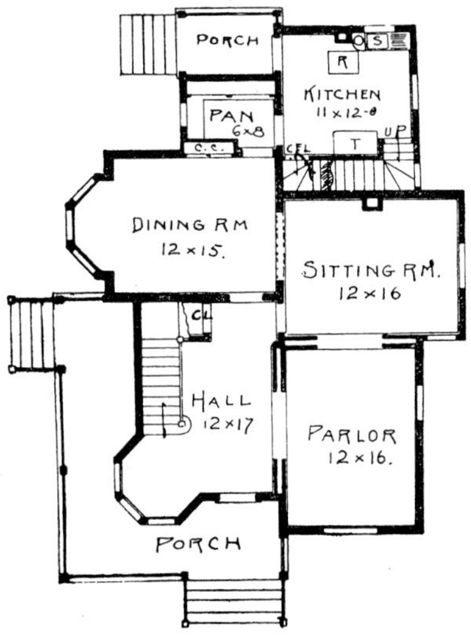

FIRST FLOOR PLAN

DESIGN No. 14-E. **RESIDENCE AT TOTTENVILLE, N. Y.** *Geo. F. Barber & Co., Arcts.*

COST, $3,000 TO $3,500

THE RESIDENCE shown herewith contains many commendable features in the arrangement of the plan. There is a cellar under kitchen and back stairs 7 feet deep. The stories are 10 feet and 9 feet 2 inches, respectively, with the hall and parlor finished in hardwoods, the rest in paint work, which is not expensive, yet is very tasteful if smoothly done. Dimensions of the ground floor are 39 x 61 feet over porches.

Especial attention is called to the large closet-room provided. The roof is shingled, sides weather-boarded and sheathed with paper between, brick foundation; but these materials may be varied according to location.

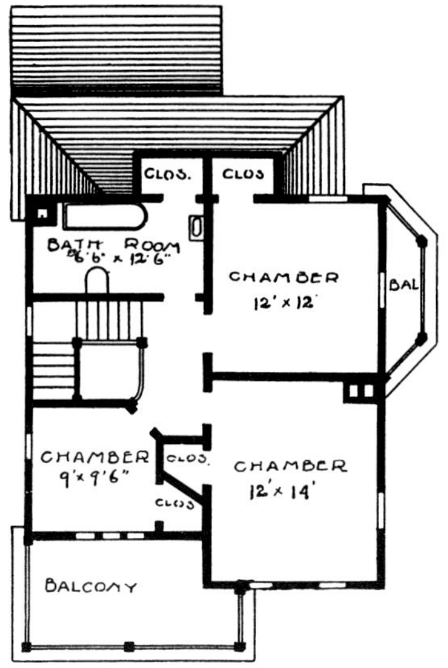

SECOND FLOOR PLAN

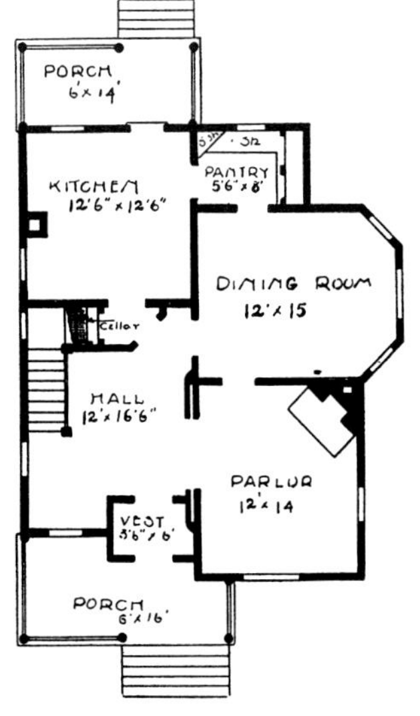

FIRST FLOOR PLAN

DESIGN No. 15-E. *Geo. F. Barber & Co., Arcts.*

A PLEASANT HOME

COST, $2,000 TO $2,400

THIS DESIGN was prepared to meet the requirements of those desiring an inexpensive house in the Colonial style. Simplicity of design, with good proportion, are the ends sought. The plan is neatly arranged for six rooms, but by slight changes in rear, where bath-room is located, another room can be had.

The cellarway is under front stairs, though back stairs can be had by enlarging the house a little for that purpose, the object being to get a good house for about $2,000. The foundation is of brick, with a small cellar. Roof shingled. Width of front, 29 feet. Stories 9 feet and 8 feet 2 inches, respectively.

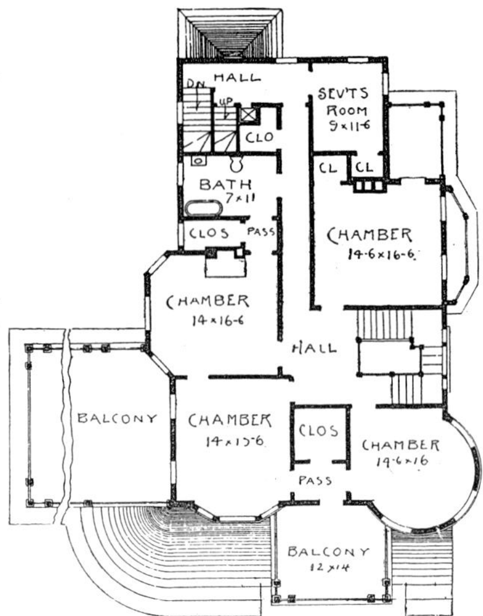

SECOND FLOOR PLAN

DESIGN No. 16-E. **A DESIRABLE COLONIAL HOME** *Geo. F. Barber & Co., Arcts.*

COST, $12,000

THE ABOVE house is of Colonial style and has many desirable features, both in plans and exterior design. The cut does not show many of its beautiful details. The interior is also of an elaborate character, the beam and column treatment being carried out in many places. All interior trims are of choice hardwoods highly finished.

Parquette floors, paneled ceiling and wainscotings are extensively used with rich effect, all in the prevailing style, Colonial. A beautiful feature of the library are the two curved bookcases built in on either side of the entrance. Slate roof, hot water heat, stone foundation, cellar under entire house. First-class in every respect. Width 49 feet, exclusive of carriage porch. Stories 10 feet and 9 feet 6 inches, respectively.

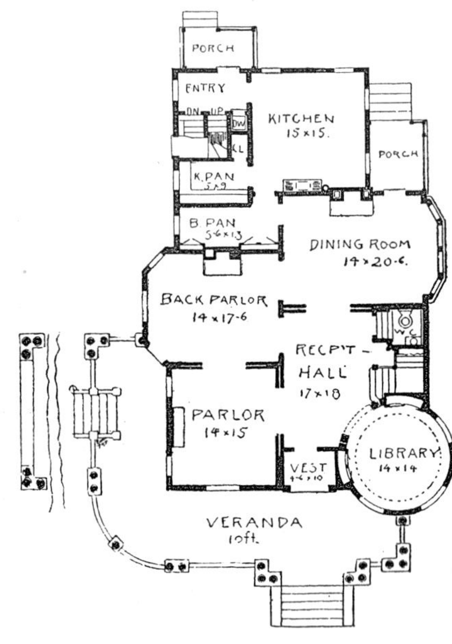

FIRST FLOOR PLAN

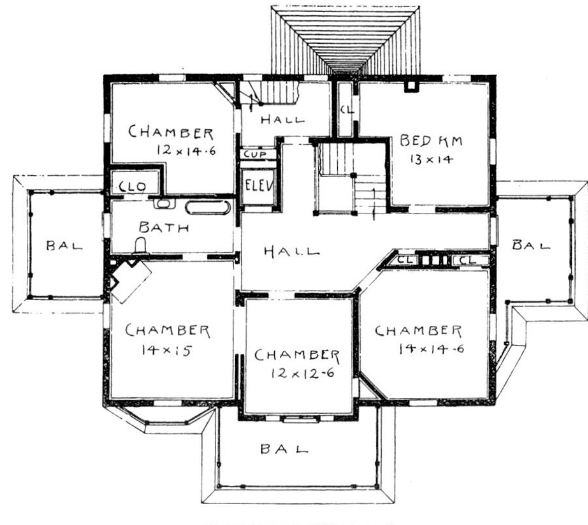

SECOND FLOOR PLAN

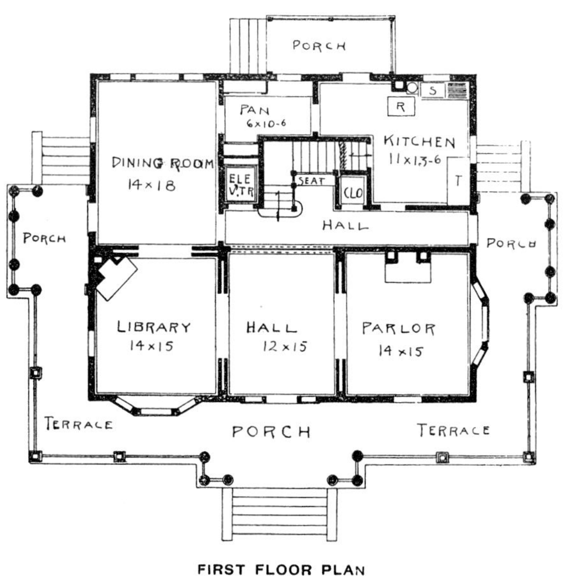

FIRST FLOOR PLAN

DESIGN No. 17-E. *Geo. F. Barber & Co., Arcts.*

AN INEXPENSIVE HOME—(COLONIAL)

COST, $3,400 TO $3,800

A PLAIN, substantial home of comparatively low cost, suitable for rather wide ground, and with a properly treated lawn will be a handsome home. The front arrangement gives a spacious effect, the centre hall being large enough for sitting-room. The grille across the hall and a neat staircase beyond, with an upholstered seat in the nook, is rich in effect. An elevator for trunks, invalids, etc., is employed. Complete in every detail.

Stories are 10 feet and 9 feet 2 inches. Width of house 49 feet over porches. Good cellar. Shingle roof.

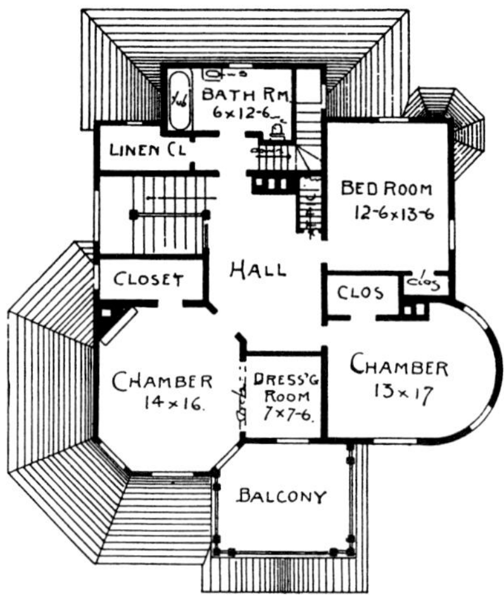

SECOND FLOOR PLAN

DESIGN No. 18-E. **RESIDENCE AT MARSHALL, MO.** *Geo. F. Barber & Co., Arcts.*

COST, $3,600 TO $4,000

THE FLOOR PLANS of this house were very carefully arranged, and one can not help but admire the entire treatment, especially the hall. A neat grille treatment between parlor and hall gives an artistic effect. Both front and side entrance are provided for the hall.

The exterior effect of the circle end of library is a beautiful feature, especially in the roof. Hardwood is liberally used for interior finish. There are also many beautiful windows in the design. Good finish is employed throughout.

The building has a frontage of 50 feet and a depth of 52 feet over porches. Stories 10 feet and 9 feet 2 inches, respectively. The second story and roof are shingled. Good cellar, brick foundation, and furnace heat.

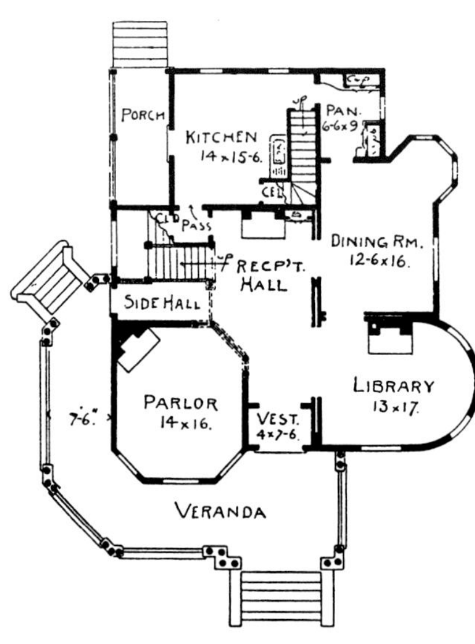

FIRST FLOOR PLAN

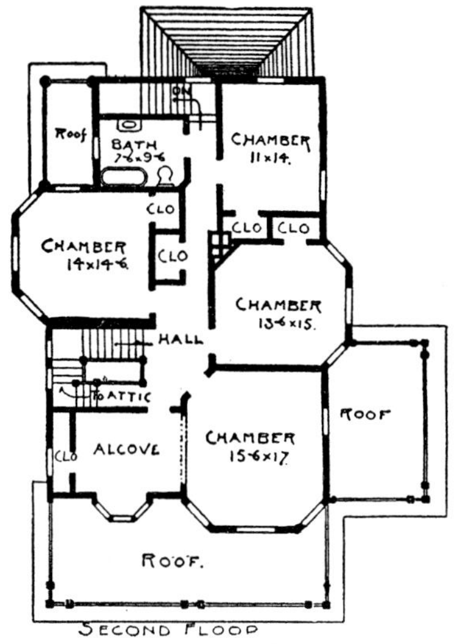

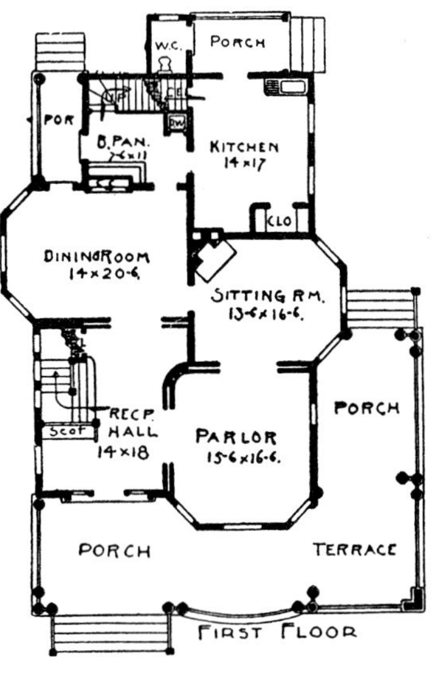

DESIGN No. 19-E.

COLONIAL RESIDENCE AT ELKADER, IOWA

Geo. F. Barber & Co., Arcts.

COST, $4,600 TO $5,200

THE above is a frame Colonial home of splendid proportions, is very compact and possesses many desirable features, such as folding doors, by which several rooms may be united. The rooms are all large and numerous. The veranda is a special feature, being large and handsomely designed. A good cellar is provided, and stone foundation, including stone for porch piers. The roof, which is simple in construction, is nicely studded with artistic dormers. The sitting-room bay extends up to the main cornice and is roofed in artistic shape. Hardwood is extensively used for interior finishing. Hardware, glass, plumbing, etc., are all good. Altogether it is a first-class home. The stories are 10 feet and 9 feet 2 inches. A Paragon furnace is the means of heating.

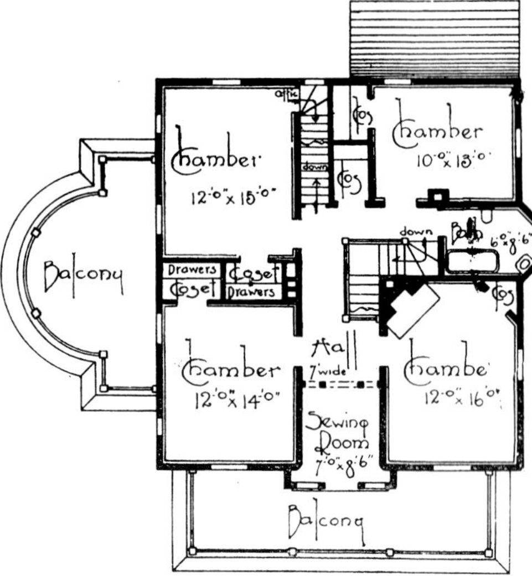

SECOND FLOOR PLAN

DESIGN No. 20-E—Ornate.

SQUARE COLONIAL HOME

Geo. F. Barber & Co., Arcts.

COST, $3,600 TO $4,000

THE ABOVE Colonial home was designed to meet the demand for something both artistic and convenient. The arrangement of the two front rooms and hall is not only convenient but beautiful in its effect. The dining-room is also an ideal room. The convenience also of the rear part of the house will be apparent.

The front porch as well as the side one are features of merit. A beautiful feature of the plan is the throwing together of the dining-room, hall, parlor and library by wide openings. With cellar under back part of house, stone foundation, shingle roof, and a generous amount of hardwood interior finish, this house can be built in almost any locality for the price given.

Width over all, 55 feet. Stories, 9 feet 6 inches and 9 feet, respectively.

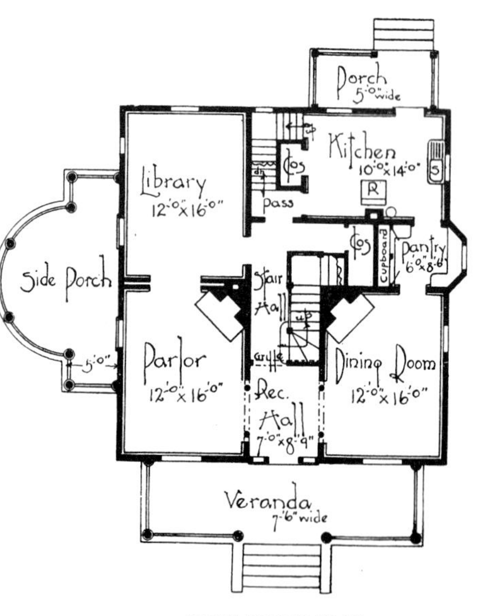

FIRST FLOOR PLAN

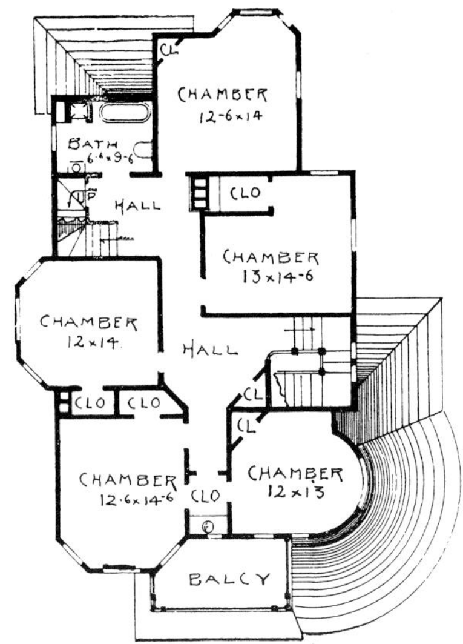

SECOND FLOOR PLAN

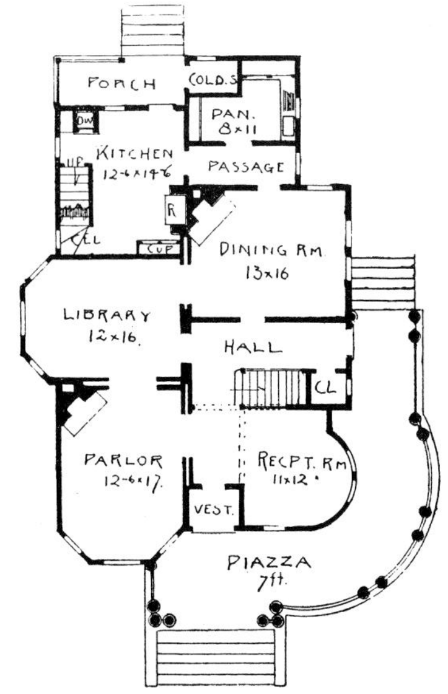

FIRST FLOOR PLAN

DESIGN No. 21-E. **A MODERN HOME IN COLONIAL RENAISSANCE** *Geo. F. Barber & Co., Arcts.*

COST, $4,000 TO $4,500

IN THE above design we have a handsome hall treatment, with connection with three principal rooms and a side entrance opening on to the porch, which extends around from the front. The lavatory, under front stairs, near side entrance, is a convenient feature. Five rooms and bath are shown on second floor.

The style is a modified Colonial, with an exterior designed to present a handsomely broken outline. The plans call for a good cellar under the entire house, with stone foundation. Furnace heat. Balance of house is finished in good shape, with slate roof, best American glass, fine hardware and suitable plumbing fixtures throughout. Width of front is 42 feet over porch. Stories, 10 feet and 9 feet, respectively.

For price of working plans see the inside front cover.

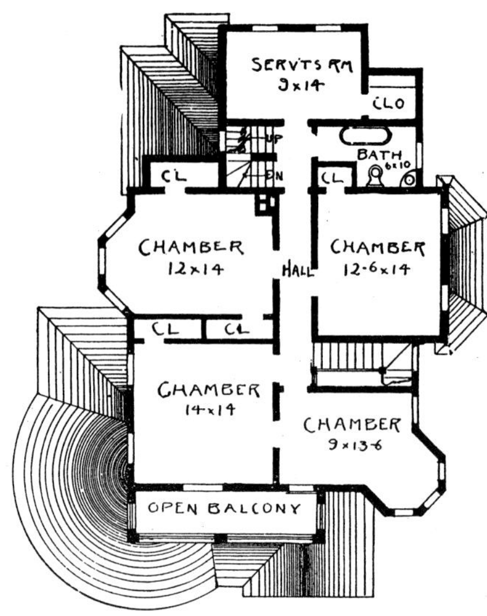

SECOND FLOOR PLAN

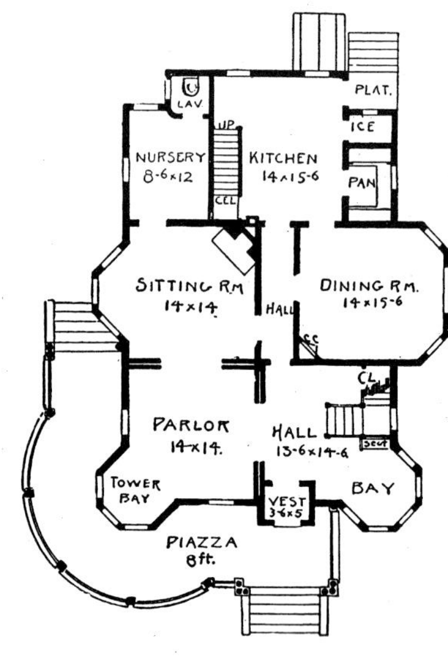

FIRST FLOOR PLAN

DESIGN No. 22-E. **RESIDENCE AT DARTSMOUTH, N. H.** *Geo. F. Barber & Co., Arcts.*

COST, $4,800 TO $5,300

THE above design is the home of one of Dartmouth's most eminent physicians. It is an elegant Colonial house for so low a price. The hall and parlor are nice rooms, and in connection with the sitting-room the combination is handsome. A narrow hall extends from the front hall to the kitchen, a very desirable feature with many housekeepers.

A cellar under the entire house is divided by brick walls into various rooms—one for furnace and fuel, another for laundry, and one for vegetables. The laundry contains three tubs. Stone is used for foundation walls; otherwise the house is of frame, with second-story, gables and roof shingled. The interior is finished mostly in hardwoods, and everything throughout is first-class. Width of front is 45 feet 7 inches over porches. Stories are 10 feet and 9 feet 2 inches, with a good attic, finished.

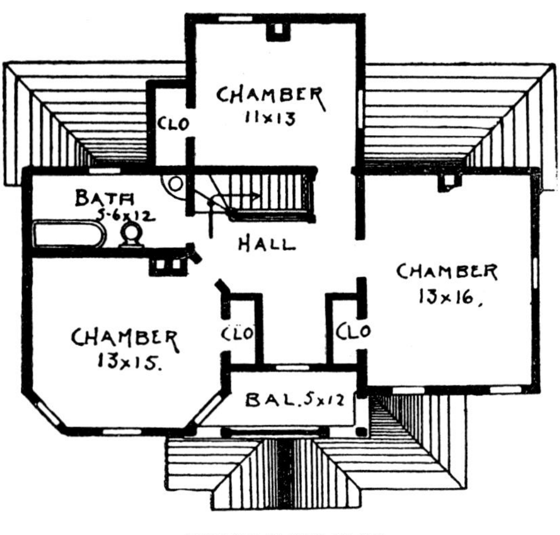

SECOND FLOOR PLAN

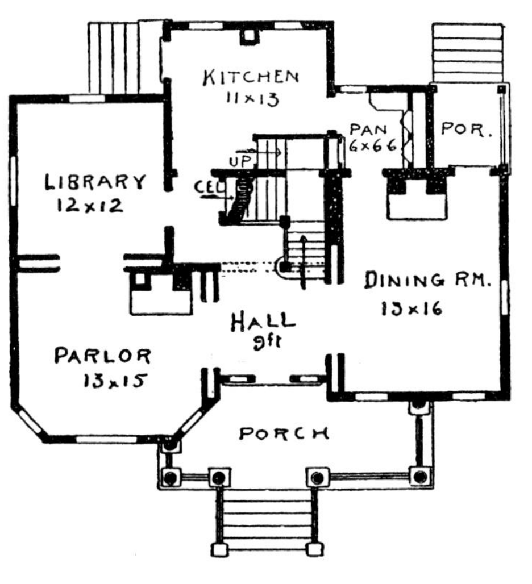

FIRST FLOOR PLAN

DESIGN No. 23-E

PERSPECTIVE VIEW

Geo. F. Barber & Co., Arcts

COST, $2,200 TO $2,400

THE above is a rather peculiar design, but is one of the most fascinating structures when built imaginable. There is a beautiful something about it not found elsewhere. The plans are for a wide lot of not much depth and are so compact and convenient they give lots of room for little money. Simple interior finish is employed to keep down cost. In many localities this house can be built for $1,500. A small cellar, shingled roof, brick foundation. Width of front is 40 feet. Stories, 10 feet, and 9 feet 2 inches.

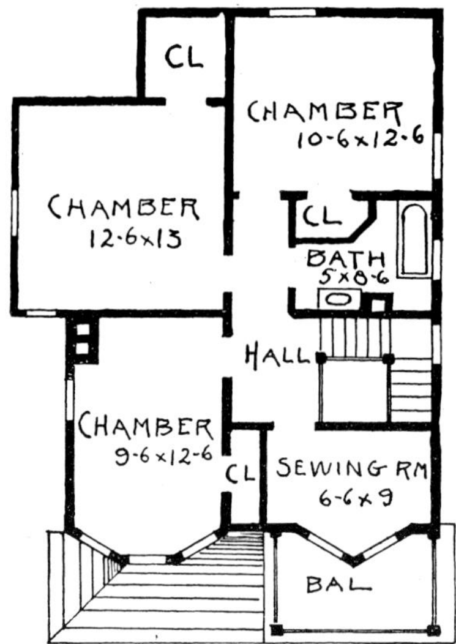

SECOND FLOOR PLAN

DESIGN No 24-E. *Geo. F. Barber & Co., Arcts.*

TASTY AND CHEAP

COST, $1,800 TO $2,000

THE ABOVE Colonial cottage was designed for a handsome home at a moderate cost. Seven rooms are provided, with many conveniences. A small cellar is provided under the hall and kitchen, with brick foundation walls. The exterior walls are weather-boarded all the way up; the roof shingled. Everything is included in the estimate for a turnkey job, with satisfactory materials all through.

The interior trimming, of course, must be simple and plain, but nicely finished. A back staircase could be had by running up from the kitchen to the landing of the front stairs. A small ice-door opens from the back porch to the ice-box in the pantry. Width of house is 25 feet 6 inches. Stories 9 feet 6 inches, and 9 feet, respectively.

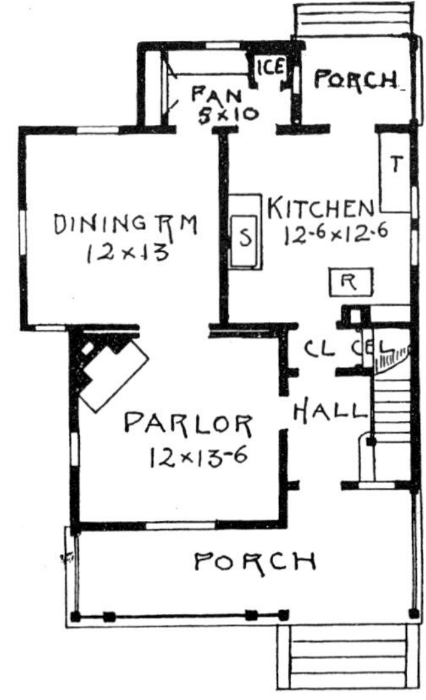

FIRST FLOOR PLAN

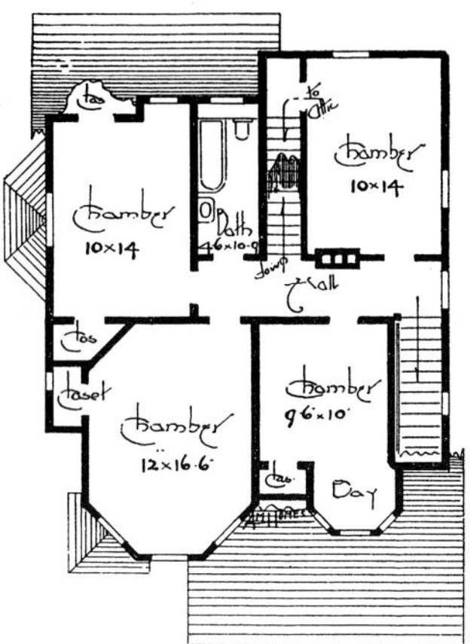

SECOND FLOOR PLAN

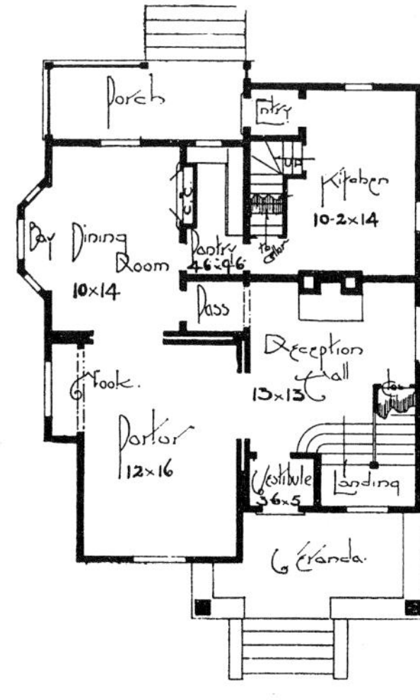

FIRST FLOOR PLAN

DESIGN No. 25-E. **RESIDENCE AT PRINCETON, ILL.** *Geo. F. Barber & Co., Arcts.*

COST, $2,800 TO $3,200

THIS attractive little cottage is in style, one of the many phases of Colonial work. The plan is compact, thus getting good room without covering much ground. As the hall is to be used as a sitting-room, the stairs were placed in the front in order to give ample space around the fire-place. The owner suggested the arrangement of the floors by rough sketches from which this house was developed, and she has included many nice features.

A good cellar, containing a furnace, etc., is provided. Weather-boarding is used on the first story with shingles on the second story and roof. Neat interior finish of inexpensive woods are used. Size 32 x 42 feet over porches. Stories are 9 feet 6 inches and 8 feet 6 inches, respectively. The price includes a furnace, plumbing, and all complete.

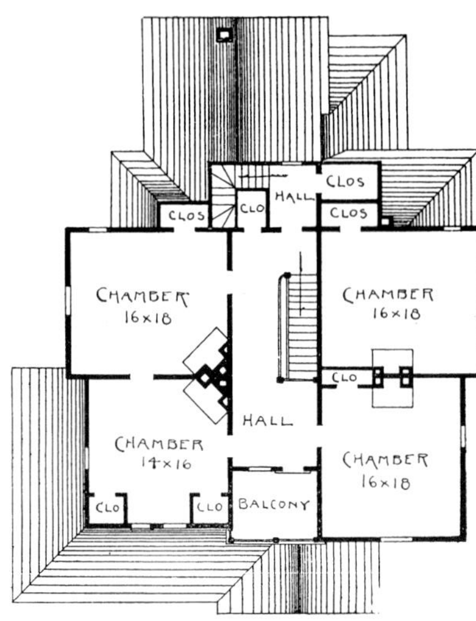

SECOND FLOOR PLAN

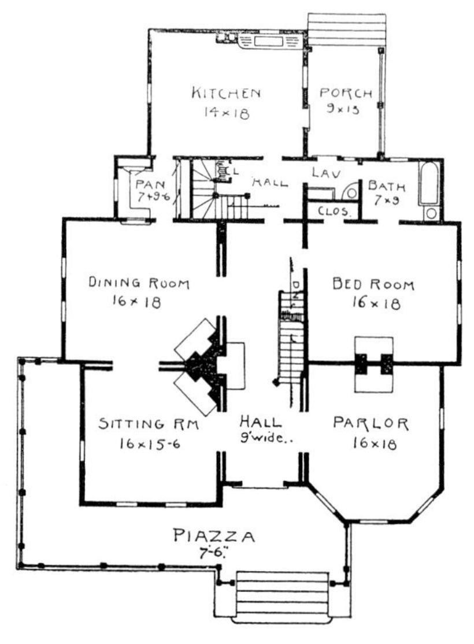

FIRST FLOOR PLAN

DESIGN No. 26-E.

RESIDENCE AT AUBURN, KY.

Geo. F. Barber & Co., Arcts.

COST, $3,500 TO $4,000

THIS has proven a very satisfactory plan for a Southern climate, and at a moderate cost. The exterior is simple and tasty. The foundation is of stone with a small cellar. The roof is covered with tin shingles of artistic yet simple pattern, giving a very pretty effect. The gables were also treated the same.

Two rooms and hall were finished in oak, the rest in bright pine, natural finish. Some very nice stonework, including steps, is worked in around the front piazza. The house has a frontage of 56 feet over porches; stories 10 feet and 9 feet, respectively. The style is simple, durable and inexpensive, and will make a most satisfactory home. A large bed-room, closet and bath-room, with a private lavatory, have been provided on the first floor.

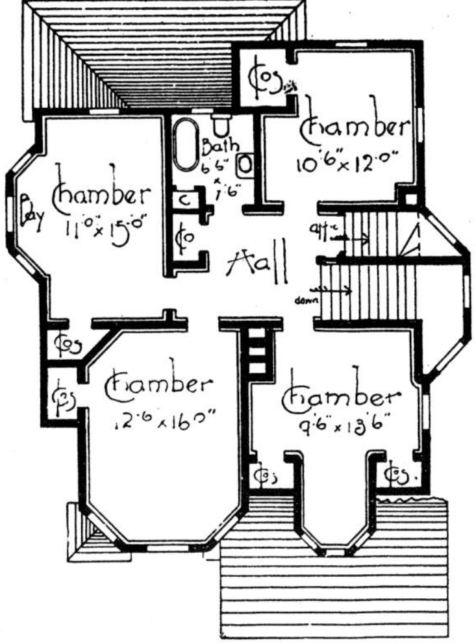

SECOND FLOOR PLAN

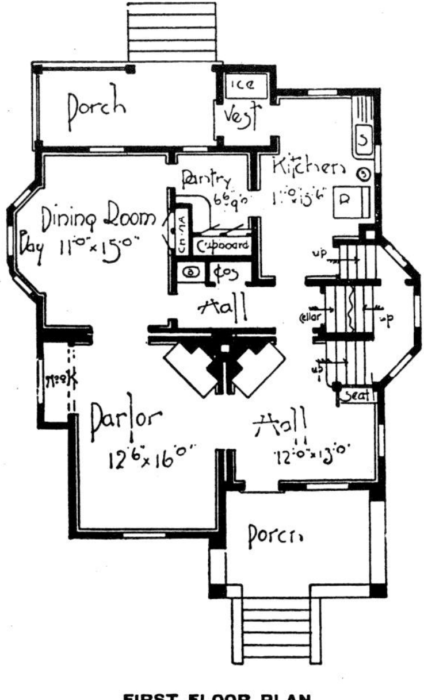

FIRST FLOOR PLAN

DESIGN No. 27-E. **RESIDENCE AT E. GREENWICH, R. I.** *Geo. F. Barber & Co., Arcts.*

COST, $3,800 TO $4,200

IT IS HARD to imagine a more cosy and compact home than this picture represents. The hall with its fire-place; the beautiful connection of the hall, parlor and dining-room; the combination stairs; the wash-bowl and coat closet in the rear hall; the pantry and kitchen arrangement; the rear vestibule for the ice-box, are all excellent features, more than are usually combined in so small a house. The second story is equally as well arranged.

The first story is weather-boarded, the rest of the house, including the roof, is shingled. Natural Tennessee pine interior finish throughout. Cellar under all of the house. Stone foundation. Size—35 feet 6 inches by 44 feet 6 inches over porches. Stories are 9 feet and 8 feet 6 inches. Cellar, 7 feet. Steam heat.

DESIGN No. 28-E. **HOUSE FOR NARROW LOT** *Geo. F. Barber & Co., Arcts.*

COST, $2,600 TO $3,000

THIS convenient home in Colonial treatment is suitable for a wide or narrow lot. Combination stairs are employed with economical effect. The small back room can be used for either a sink-room or for the refrigerator. Pantry and cupboard-room is especially abundant.

With cellar under kitchen, stone foundation, shingled roof and good construction, this house can be built for the price named in most localities, but will vary from this in some States. Furnace heat is used, and good glass, plumbing and hardware are employed. Width, 27 feet; stories, 9 feet 6 inches, and 9 feet, respectively.

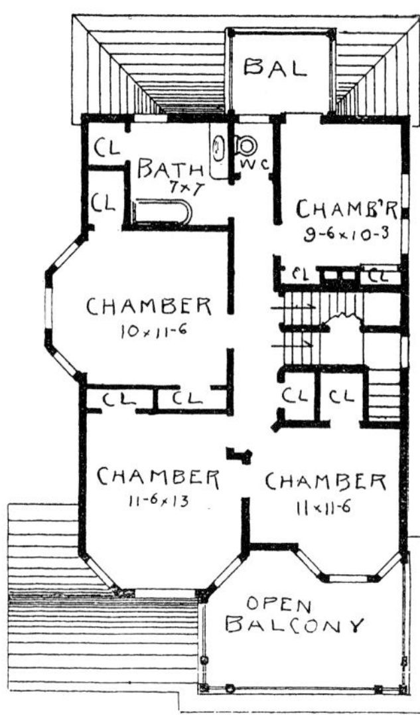

SECOND FLOOR PLAN

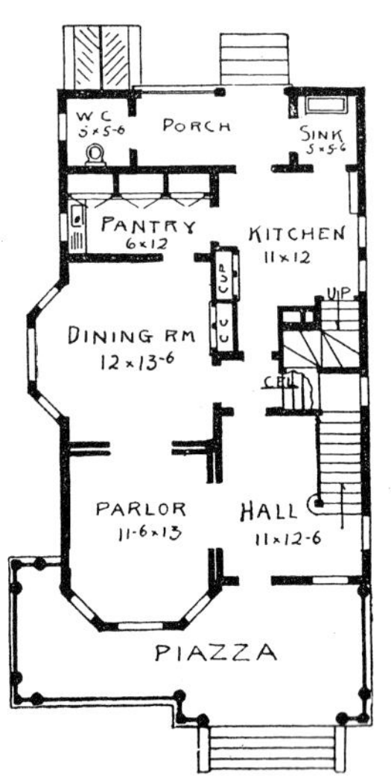

FIRST FLOOR PLAN

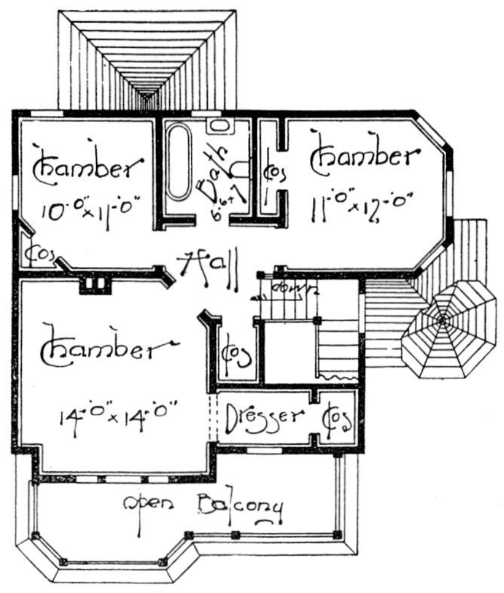

SECOND FLOOR PLAN

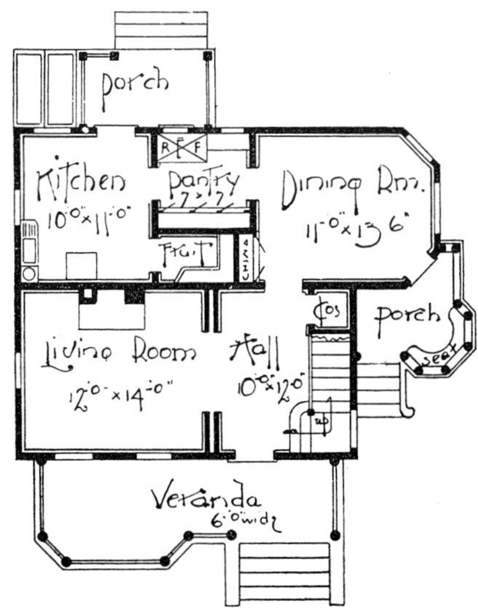

FIRST FLOOR PLAN

DESIGN No. 29-E. **A SNUG LITTLE HOME** *Geo. F. Barber & Co., Archts.*

COST, $2,400 TO $2,700

THIS charming little home has a number of unique features, both in plan of rooms and design and arrangement of porches. The neat little side porch gives access to the dining-room, besides the door from the living-room and from the kitchen; the ingle nook can be made a comfortable as well as a very artistic feature by a simple treatment in grille and seats.

The house is to be heated by a furnace, but other methods can be provided if necessary. We have combination stairs, with back stairs cut off from kitchen by a door.

The style is Colonial, and will be found highly artistic when built. Exterior material is all wood; no slate. Interior is of neat pine. Width, 31 feet. Stories 9 feet and 8 feet 2 inches. Can be built in Knoxville for $2,000. For prices of working plans see the inside front cover.

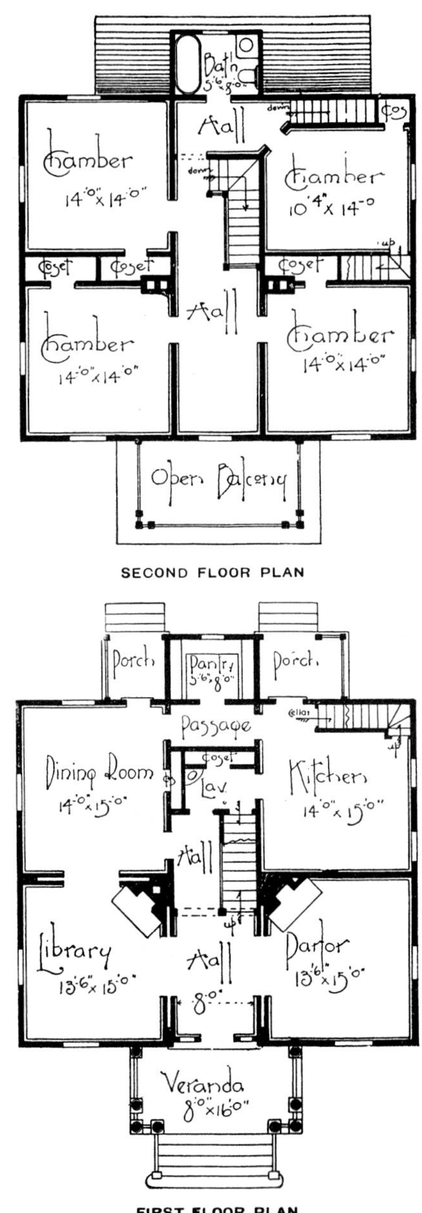

SECOND FLOOR PLAN

FIRST FLOOR PLAN

DESIGN No. 30-E. **RESIDENCE AT LEBANON, OHIO** *Geo. F. Barber & Co., Arcts.*

COST, $2,800 TO $3,200

A SQUARE, plain, Colonial home, with good cellar under entire house. Furnace heat. Two front rooms finished in oak, balance in natural pine. A special feature of the plan is the lavatory and coat closet in rear of hall under the stairs.

With our specifications we give a list of appropriate Colonial colors for outside painting. Size of house, exclusive of front porch, is 38 feet by 37 feet 6 inches. The stories are 10 feet and 8 feet 6 inches, respectively. Where simplicity is desired, this house will be found to meet those requirements.

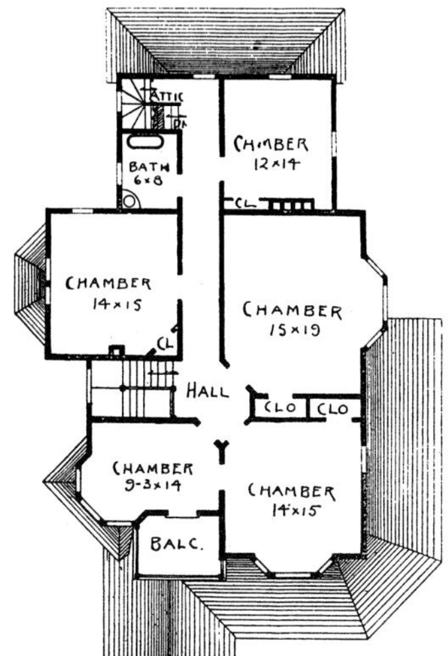

SECOND FLOOR PLAN

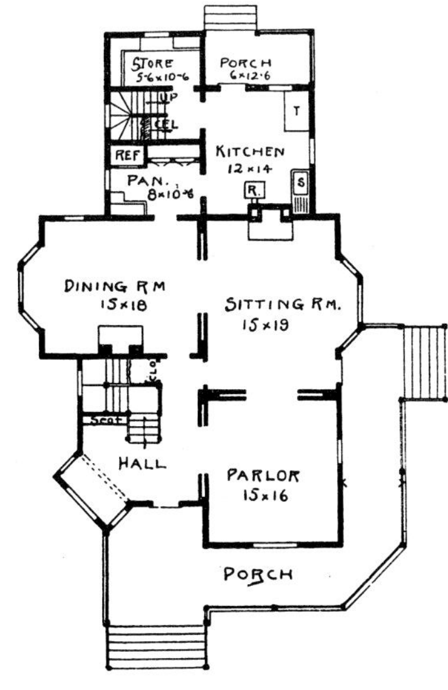

FIRST FLOOR PLAN

DESIGN No. 31-E. *Geo. F. Barber & Co., Arcts.*

A BEAUTIFUL MODERN HOME

COST, $3,400 TO $3,800

THIS PLAN shows a very popular arrangement of a handsome home at a price within reach of many, as to cost. A pavilion on the porch corner would harmonize beautifully with the other features. Five splendid rooms are shown in the above plan with closets, bath-room, etc. The handsome front bay, the tower, the balcony, are special features in this design.

A house of this style will always appear well on any street, and with grounds in harmony would be a most delightful place to spend one's days. A good cellar is provided. Stone foundation, shingled roof. Furnace heat is arranged for, though not included in the estimate. Good glass, plumbing and hardware are also provided for. Width over porch 48 feet. Stories 10 feet and 9 feet 2 inches.

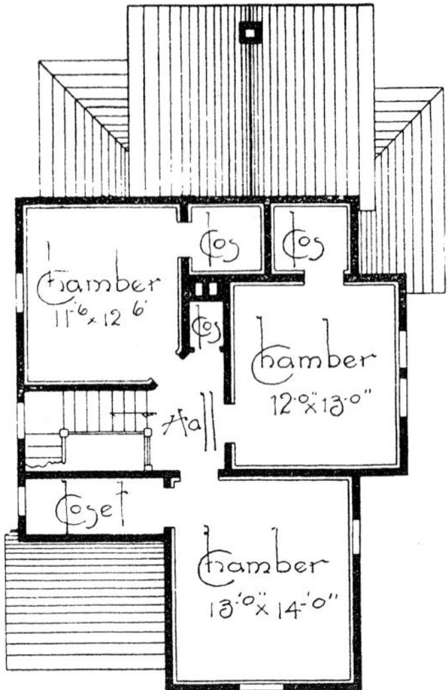

SECOND FLOOR PLAN

DESIGN No. 32-E. **A MODEL COTTAGE** *Geo. F. Barber & Co., Arcts.*

COST, IN FRAME, $1,600 TO $1,800
COST, IN BRICK, $1,800 TO $2,000

THIS LITTLE HOME, erected a number of times, is a model home, one and one-half stories, cellar under entire house. Second story, gables and roof are shingled. Furnace heat usually used. Paint work is used for the interior in all except the parlor and dining-room, which have woodwork of varnished pine.

Width, 28 feet 3 inches; length, 47 feet 3 inches over porches. Stories are 9 feet and 8 feet 3 inches. Foundation may be of stone or brick, as desired. This cottage can be worked nicely with first story or both in brick veneer, but the best appearance is with only the first story so treated, shingling the second story.

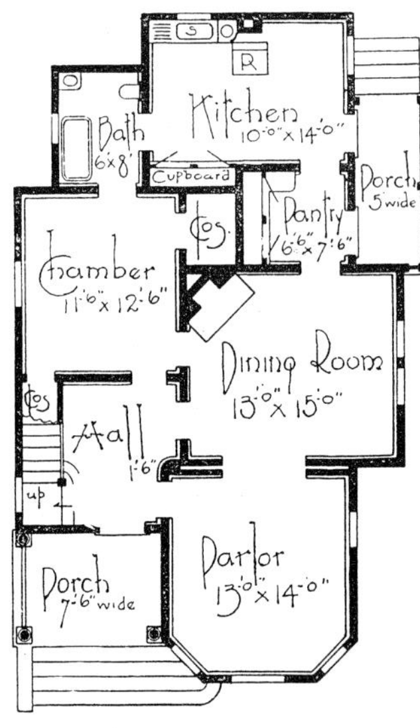

FIRST FLOOR PLAN

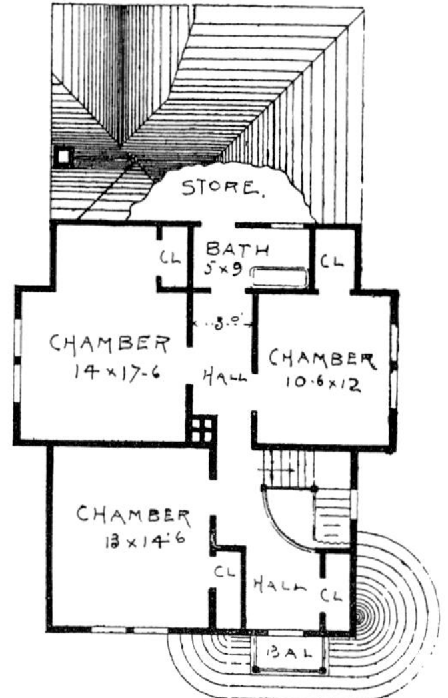

SECOND FLOOR PLAN

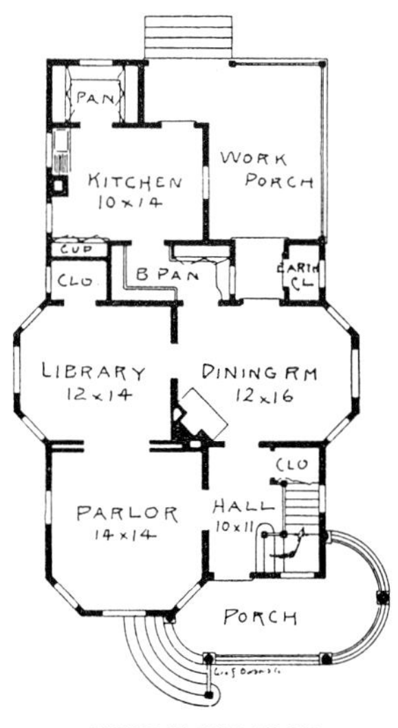

FIRST FLOOR PLAN

DESIGN No. 33-E. **COTTAGE AT CLARA, O. T.** *Geo. F. Barber & Co., Arcts.*

COST, $1,800 TO $2,000

THE ABOVE COTTAGE was recently erected at Clara, O. T., and has many artistic as well as convenient features. The porch especially is nice, plain, very neat and original in design. There is no cellar provided for, but one may be had at a very slight additional cost. The foundation is of brick; the roof and gables are shingled; the rest is sheathed, papered and weather-boarded. The interior is mostly paint work, except the hall and three principal rooms, which are finished in natural pine.

The general design will commend it for almost any locality. Width of front is 32 feet, exclusive of porch extensions. Stories are 9 feet 6 inches, and 8 feet, respectively.

DESIGN No. 34-E. *Geo. F. Barber & Co., Arcts.*

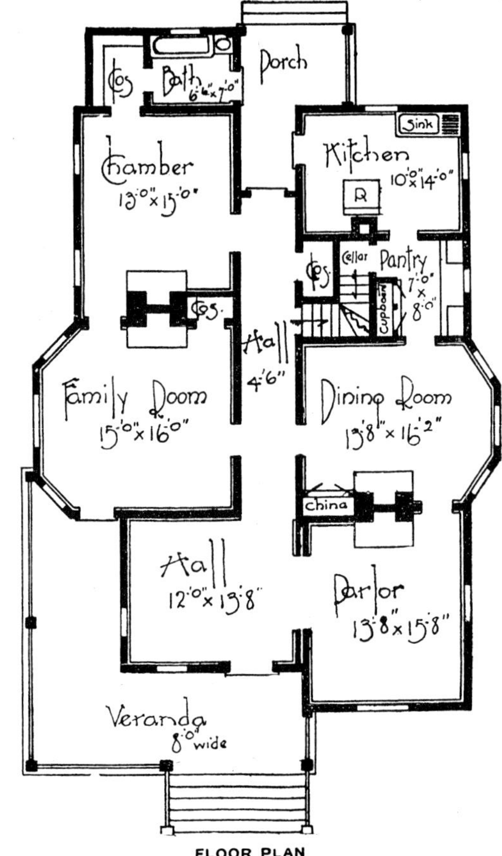

FLOOR PLAN

RESIDENCE OF MRS. J. W. TAYLOR, KNOXVILLE, TENN.

COST, $1,500 TO $1,600

THIS neat cottage was recently erected in Knoxville for $1,500, including mantels and grates complete, plumbing and sewer connections, two rooms finished in attic. There is no basement, but a substantial brick foundation. Handsome windows, and all of first floor finished in natural pine. No paint work of any kind. The roof is shingled, as also the gables.

The exterior painting is of light cream with dark buff trimmings. A beautiful building in every particular, one of especial convenience. Width of front, 35 feet. Story, 10 feet high.

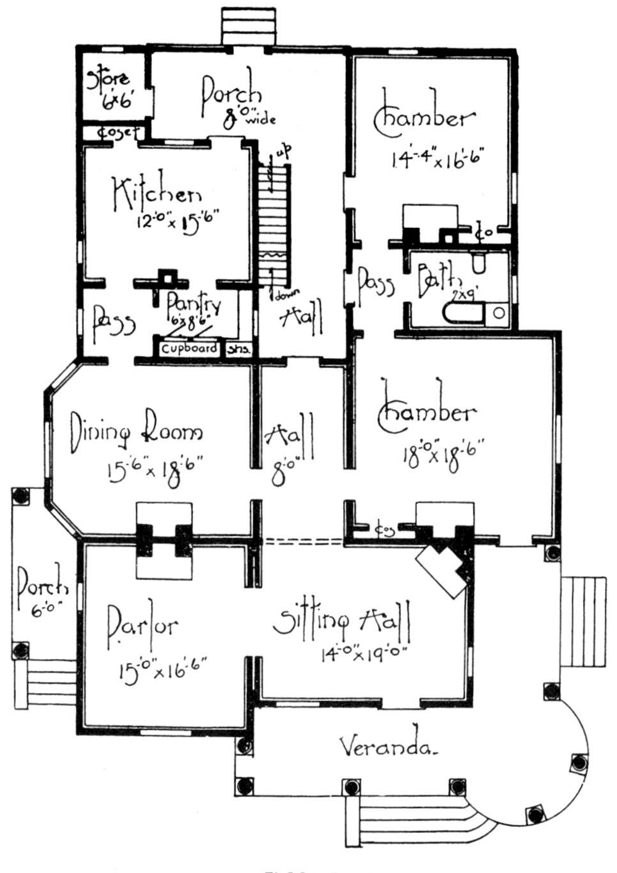

FLOOR PLAN

DESIGN No. 35-E. **ONE-STORY COLONIAL COTTAGE** *Geo. F. Barber & Co., Arcts.*

COST. $2,000 TO $2,200

THIS one-story Colonial cottage has many conveniences, and shows how this style may be applied to homes of low cost. It was designed for a lady in a Southern State, and so pleased her that it called forth a letter expressing her admiration. The porch columns are large and used without a balustrade between them, a very characteristic feature of this style.

There are six rooms on the first floor, including the reception hall, besides a bath, pantry, closet, etc. The attic can be reached by a convenient stair case in the rear part of the hall and good rooms finished if necessary. The width of house over porches is 50 feet, length 64 feet. Story, 10 feet 6 inches high. By the employment of a competent architect on such work, you get so much better results that his charges are not a consideration. By his services you get greater convenience, better design, better construction, better material, and best of all, a much better home.

DESIGN No. 36-E. *Geo. F. Barber & Co., Arcts.*

HARD TO BEAT

COST, $2,400 TO $2,600

IT IS hard to imagine a home more beautiful than this one from every point of view. It has been built in every state in the Union, thus showing its adaptability to all climates. The three main front rooms and hall are in oak with paneled wainscoting in the hall; all other rooms are in natural pine.

For a home with an elegant hall and five splendid rooms, besides pantry, bath-room, closets, etc., on the first floor and three good rooms in the attic this home is certainly "hard to beat." A small cellar is provided to be used for heater and vegetables.

The entire house is weather-boarded except the gables, which are shingled. The roof is also shingled. There is an art glass circle transom in the central part of the tripple window in the dining-room. The dimensions are width 50 feet, depth 58 feet. Stories are 10 feet 6 inches and 9 feet. All finished very completely throughout.

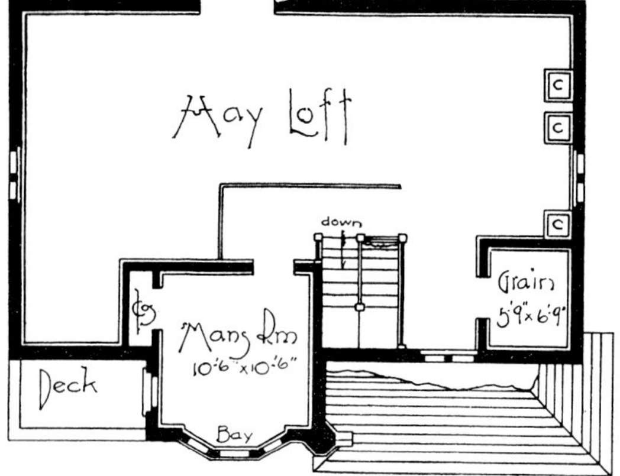

SECOND FLOOR PLAN

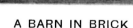

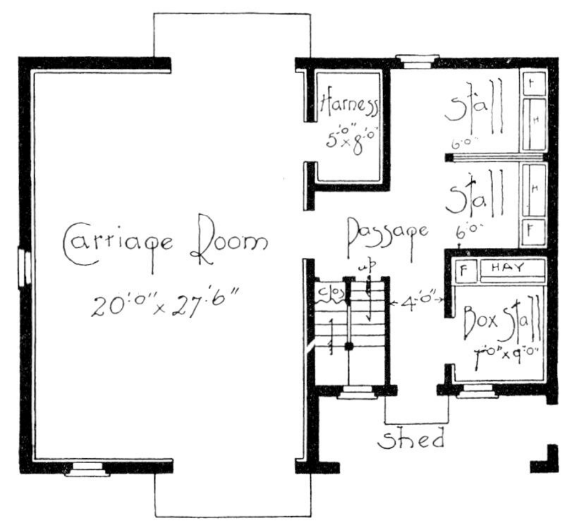

FIRST FLOOR PLAN

DESIGN No. 37-E. *Geo. F. Barber & Co., Arcts.*

A BARN IN BRICK

COST, IN BRICK, $1,800 TO $2,000---IN FRAME, $1,300 TO $1,500

IN PLANNING a barn, certain individual requirements are necessary, as to cost, location, frontage, number of vehicles, number of horses or cows, number of single and box stables, etc. With this information at hand we can prepare plans to suit any requirement. Let us plan your barn when we plan your residence; the harmony will be better.

The above illustration shows a barn in brick, and with slight changes it can be carried out in frame. The roof is shingled, but for better service and appearance slate could be substituted, and for the most lasting and beautiful effect red clay tile for the roof is recommended. The tile would also be in excellent keeping with the style of the building. A light slat screen some four feet high, built in the hay loft as shown, keeps the hay from the door of the man's room and from the stairs.

We present this design as a single example of our work in this line, but we prepare designs for such buildings to be in harmony with the other buildings; yet this style will harmonize beautifully with most any substantial, Colonial, Romanesque or English residence. Size—38 feet wide by 29 feet deep.

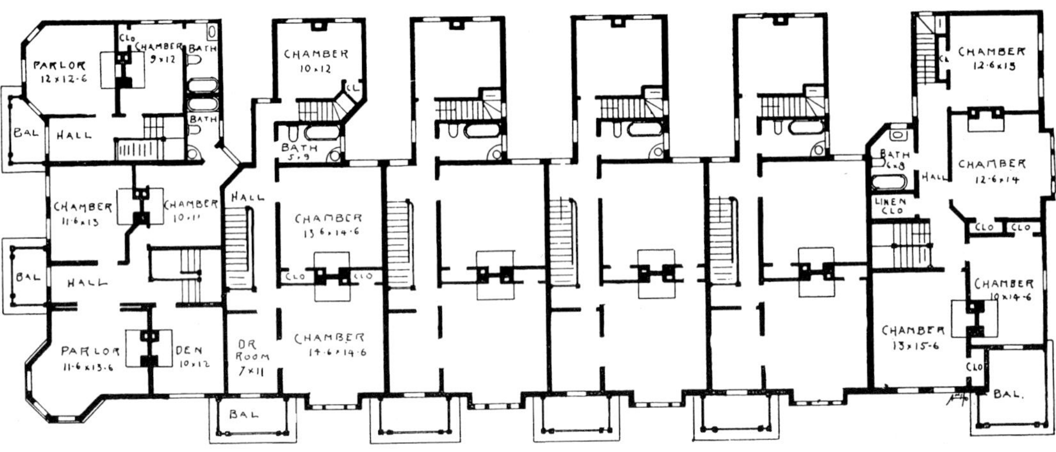

SECOND FLOOR PLANS

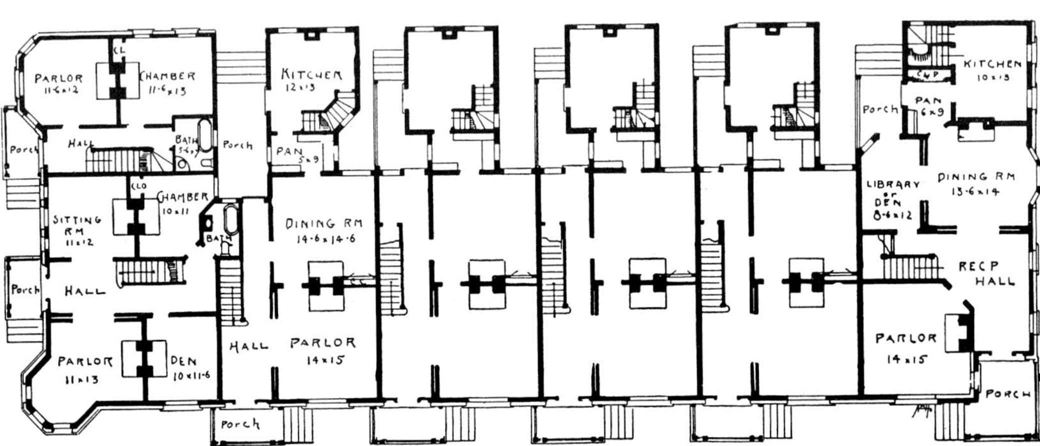

FIRST FLOOR PLANS

FLOOR PLANS FOR DESIGN No. 38-E

DESIGN No. 38-E. **A HANDSOME TENEMENT BLOCK** *Geo. F. Barber & Co., Arcts.*

THIS BLOCK of tenements contains a number of living apartments, which have been so planned as to be changed or shifted to suit many different requirements. Brick and slate are the materials for the exterior, though wood may be used. Entire length 145 feet. Most of this block is provided with kitchens and all complete for family's use entire, and some for families who board out but wish good, comfortable living apartments. Further particulars on application.

THE USES to which grilles may be applied are many. They embellish and enliven as nothing else can. They make odd corners and unsightly nooks places of beauty. They come in as oases in a barren desert. The form, design and character of such ornaments are illimitable. See if you can not think of some place where you can utilize some one of these designs.

GRILLE SCHEME FOR A NARROW HALL

Grilles are purely ornamental, but when designed and executed as they should be, surpass all other forms of ornament. The grille softens and mellows the harsh, stiff proportions possessed by so many rooms. They remove the cold and repulsive character of apartments, which all other attempts at decoration have failed to do.

GRILLE EMBELLISHMENT FOR A BAY WINDOW

The many places to which these neat and inexpensive ornaments can be applied make them useful studies. They inspire the beholder with a sense of refinement and taste of the highest character.

COLONIAL FRONT DOOR, SHOWING PLAIN AND BEVELED PLATE GLASS WITH METAL BARS

GRILLE SUITABLE FOR A HALL OR OTHER WIDE OPENING

No matter what the shape or condition of the place, a grille can be designed to fit and relieve even the most unsightly corner. Very few can, however, design a grille properly; the tendency is to get them too heavy and clumsy.